The Ghost of Bellamy Bridge

Ten Stories of Ghosts & Monsters
from Jackson County, Florida

Dale Cox

2012

ISBN-13: 978-0615740515
ISBN-10: 0615740510

Visit the author online at:

www.exploresouthernhistory.com

Old Kitchen Books
4523 Oak Grove Road
Bascom, Florida 32423

The woman said, "I see a spirit coming up out of the ground."
"What does he look like?" he asked.
"An old man wearing a robe is coming up," she said.
Then Saul knew it was Samuel, and he bowed down and prostrated himself with his face to the ground.
Samuel said to Saul, "Why have you disturbed me by bringing me up?"
1 Samuel 28: 13-15

This book is respectfully dedicated to
Sue Tindel & Robert Earl Standland.

Thank you both so much for the help and encouragement
you gave during the research and writing of this volume.

Table of Contents

Section One

Section Two

Introduction

The story of the Ghost of Bellamy Bridge is one of Florida's best known and most intriguing legends. Like most ghost stories, it revolves around the collective memory of tragic events and has been preserved by word of mouth and occasional newspaper articles for more than 170 years. In the case of this story, however, there is much more to the tale than meets the eye. In fact, the legend of the Ghost of Bellamy Bridge is as much a historical and cultural artifact as it is a tale of the supernatural. For the historian and lover of literature it provides an opportunity to look back through the mists of time and touch the lives of people and a famous novelist who lived and died more than one century ago. For the lover of chilling tales of things that go bump in the night, it is the real thing, a ghost story that has not just one, but possibly as many as four ghosts.

Elizabeth and Samuel Bellamy were real people of the 19th century, as was novelist Caroline Lee Hentz, who would play a strange and surprising role in preserving the memory of their lives. Samuel was one of the architects of Florida's original constitution and his work at the Constitutional Convention of 1838 helped assure statehood for the old Spanish colony. Elizabeth was the daughter of an American general of the War of 1812 and the granddaughter of patriots who defended North Carolina from the British during the American Revolution. Mrs. Hentz was a preeminent novelist of her day, the author of the Southern rebuttal to *Uncle Tom's Cabin* and one of the bestselling writers of her time. The three would come together in a bizarre set of circumstances to create a legend that lingers to this day.

The tale of Elizabeth's ghost and the haunting at Bellamy Bridge is a centerpiece of the folklore of Florida's third oldest county. Jackson County, in fact, is said to be haunted by an impressive array of ghosts, monsters and creatures of the night. For example, a mysterious apparition haunts the beautiful old Ely-Criglar House in Marianna. A little known ghost said to take the form of a beautiful young woman, the spirit antagonizes a "ghost hunting" dog named Beau and has appeared to residents of the mansion for decades.

There are strange "spook lights" in Graceville, the ghosts of murdered convicts near Cottondale, headless Indian chiefs in Sneads and an entire haunted ghost town at Old Parramore. And then there is the story of the Wild Man of Ocheesee Pond. A strange creature covered with hair and unable to communicate with his captors, he was taken from the swamps of Ocheesee Pond in the 1890s and apparently wound up at what was then the state asylum in Chattahoochee. In his grave may be the answer to the mystery of whether Bigfoot is a real creature or merely a colorful myth.

There are other stories as well, stories of a Confederate volunteer who continues to fight his last battle, of a wealthy businessman who still haunts the house he loved and of the bizarre Two Egg Stump Jumper that appears in the headlights of cars driving the dirt roads of eastern Jackson County late at night. These tales reflect the culture and heritage of one of Florida's most special places. They have their roots in the stories that our ancestors told by the light of their fireplaces on cold winter nights long ago. They are a part of who we are and remind us that the unseen world is always there, just beyond the reach of our outstretched hands.

I am often asked whether I believe in ghosts. I always answer first that 99 percent of the events and stories that people attribute to the supernatural can be explained in some scientific or natural way. It is the remaining one percent, however, that sparks my curiosity and imagination.

To answer the question of whether ghosts are real, I always encourage the curious to look in the Bible for answers and point them to the book of 1 Samuel, Chapter 28. There can be found the story of King Saul, the Witch of Endor and the ghost of the Prophet Samuel:

7. Then said Saul unto his servants: 'Seek me a woman that divineth by a ghost, that I may go to her and inquire of her.' And his servants said to him: 'Behold, there is a woman that divineth by a ghost at En-dor.

8. And Saul disguised himself, and put on other raiment, and went, he and two men with him, and they came to the woman by night; and he said: 'Divine unto me, I pray thee, by a ghost, and bring me up whomsoever I shall name unto thee.'

9. And the woman said unto him: 'Behold, thou knowest what Saul hath done, how he hath cut off those that divine by a ghost or a familiar spirit out of the land; wherefore then layest thou a snare for my life, to cause me to die?'

X

10. And Saul swore to her by the Lord, saying: 'As the Lord liveth, there shall no punishment happen to thee for this thing.'

11. Then said the woman: 'Whom shall I bring up unto thee?' And he said: 'Bring me up Samuel.'

12. And when the woman saw Samuel, she cried with a loud voice; and the woman spoke to Saul, saying: 'Why hast thou deceived me? for thou art Saul.'

13. And the king said unto her: 'Be not afraid; for what seest thou?' And the woman said unto Saul: 'I see a godlike being coming up out of the earth.'

14. And he said unto her: 'What form is he of?' And she said: 'An old man cometh up; and he is covered with a robe.' And Saul perceived that it was Samuel, and he bowed with his face to the ground, and prostrated himself.

The ghost of Samuel, however, did not give King Saul the advice he so desperately sought. Instead, Samuel berated him for having disturbed his rest and questioned why Saul would seek advice from him when God had already turned his face away from the king. He warned that God would take Saul's kingdom from him and turn it over to David and that Saul and his sons would die the next day.

The lesson of this ghost story from the Bible is clear. Ghosts are real, but it is extremely unwise to consult with them, for they can offer nothing that God himself has not already given or taken away. There is great wisdom in 1 Samuel 28 of which those who seek to open a channel of communication with the dead should take heed. I often think of this chapter when people inquire of me whether I have ever tried to use a recorder to communicate with a ghost. I always answer with an emphatic "No."

Preserving and enjoying stories of ghosts as folklore and legend, however, is very different from trying to communicate with spirits. The telling of these tales has been part of human culture for thousands of years and they tell us much about the attempts by our ancestors to explain the mysterious and macabre.

I hope you will enjoy the stories that follow in the "spirit" (pun intended) they are intended. They are some of the most fascinating tales that I have heard of from Jackson County and I've attempted to dig into the real history of each to find out if the facts match the legends. I believe you will find that the results of these investigations make for fascinating reading.

I am very grateful to a number of people for making this book possible. Thank you especially to Sue Tindel and Robert Earl Standland from the office of Jackson County Clerk of Courts Dale Guthrie. They helped me tremendously in my efforts to dig through the county's historical records in search of information on the real stories behind the legends. Thank you also to Ms. Guthrie for providing such valuable assistance to researchers and the general public by hiring such outstanding employees.

I also must express my appreciation to my sons, William Cox and Alan Cox. They have served as my sounding board for many years and both participated materially in the effort to save and preserve Bellamy Bridge for future generations.

Chuck Hatcher and Pam Fuqua deserve the recognition of all who read this for the leadership role they have taken in preserving and interpreting the historical and natural resources of Jackson County, including Bellamy Bridge. Chuck is the Director of Jackson County Parks and has supervised the building of the Bellamy Bridge Heritage Trail which once again provides public access to the historic bridge. Pam is the Director of Tourism for Jackson County and has served as a volunteer tour guide at Bellamy Bridge. She has been instrumental in the promotion of the bridge as a tourism resource.

Thanks also are due to the employees of the Jackson County Parks Department and the employees and inmates from the Jackson County Correctional Facility for their work in helping to build the Bellamy Bridge Heritage Trail. The many volunteers of the Friends of Bellamy Bridge assisted in the project and much credit is due to all of them. Special recognition is given to Bill Cleckley, Faith Eidse and the staff and board members of the Northwest Florida Water Management District for their support and oversight of the Bellamy Bridge Heritage Trail project; Ted Lakey, County Administrator, and the Board of County Commissioners of Jackson County for their support of the heritage trail; the Jackson County Tourist Development Council; J-Trans, and the many others who have assisted in the development of the trail.

Ruth and Larry Kinsolving graciously welcomed me into the Ely-Criglar House and shared with me the stories of their resident ghost. They are wonderful people and each is a tremendous asset to their community. Thank you also to Beau for allowing your story and photographs to appear in this volume.

Many others too numerous to name have assisted me in one way or another through the years in the writing of this book. Thank you to all.

May God bless and keep you.

Dale Cox
2012

The Ghost of Bellamy Bridge

*Ten Stories of Ghosts & Monsters
from Jackson County, Florida*

Section One

The Ghost of Bellamy Bridge

Chapter One

The Ghost of Bellamy Bridge

It is perhaps Florida's best known ghost story. For more than 100 years, residents of Jackson County have held that the deep swamps of the Chipola River are haunted by a restless and earthbound spirit. The ghost always appears in the vicinity of Bellamy Bridge, a rusting steel-frame structure north of Marianna, not far from which can be found the overgrown and neglected grave of a young woman who died more than 175 years ago.

Her name in life was Elizabeth Jane Bellamy and the tellers of such tales say that she was one of the most beautiful young women of her day. The much loved daughter of a prominent North Carolina family, she was the bride of Dr. Samuel C. Bellamy, who was the son of another of North Carolina's most prominent families. The story of their courtship could have been taken from the pages of a romance novel and their journey to Florida is said to have been one of great adventure and high hopes.

All of their dreams and adventures collapsed in unspeakable tragedy when Samuel and Elizabeth reached Florida, a tragedy was so deep and intense that it reaches through nearly two centuries of time to touch the cultural fabric of the community even today.

The story of the Ghost of Bellamy Bridge is a legend. And as is the case with all such legends, there are numerous variations of the story. Each one is as unique and creative as mind of the story teller who repeats it, but a common thread runs through all. Samuel and Elizabeth, it has been handed down from generation to generation, were deeply in love and their romance was one of those that has quickened hearts down through the ages. Their wedding was the social event of the year, attending by the highest levels of antebellum aristocracy. The hours that followed ended in a horror of fire and screams, but even death could not end the love that had been kindled in their two young hearts.

The most popular version of the story holds that Elizabeth Jane Croom and Samuel C. Bellamy were the children of noted North Carolina families. Elizabeth, or "Betsy" as she was affectionately called, was the daughter and granddaughter of heroes of the War of 1812 and American Revolution. Her father, General William Croom, was a prosperous planter and political leader who was one of the most respected men in his state. Samuel's family was equally positioned in the social strata of the antebellum South. He held a degree in medicine from the University of Pennsylvania and was a young man schooled in Latin, Greek and the classics. Both were accustomed to the finest clothes and possessions

Samuel's brother, Dr. Edward C. Bellamy, had courted and married Elizabeth's sister, Ann Croom. The marriage strengthened the ties between the two families and dramatically increased the interest of both in the new U.S. Territory of Florida.

Hardy Bryan Croom, the brother of Ann and Elizabeth, had already moved to Florida where he was operating a large plantation on the west side of the Apalachicola River in Jackson County. One of the most prominent and noteworthy Floridians of his time, Hardy was a well-educated gentlemen who possessed a deep interest in botany and science. On one of his trips from Tallahassee back to his plantation south of present-day Sneads, he noticed an unusual tree growing in the steephead ravines of Alum Bluff in western Gadsden County.

Locals called this tree the "stinking cedar" because of the pungent odor it gave off when its bark was bruised. The wood was extremely weather resistant, so they used it to build fences and to make wooden roofing shingles. Possibly because it shed water so well, a legend grew among the people living on the Apalachicola that the "stinking cedar" was really the gopher wood from which Noah had built the ark.

The longer Hardy Croom studied the unique tree, the more he began to realize that he had never seen another quite like it. It occurred to him that he had discovered a completely new species and he named it the *Torreya taxifolia* after Dr. John Torrey, a famed botanist of his day. It turned out that Croom was right and his identification of the Florida Torreya was one of the greatest botanical discoveries of the 19th century. It still clings to life along the bluffs and ravines of the Apalachicola River and is one of the rarest trees in the world.

Hardy Bryan Croom loved Florida and his enthusiasm soon bubbled over into the hearts and minds of his family members. His father and other relatives invested heavily in land holdings in the new territory and his brother-in-law, Dr. Edward C. Bellamy, became obsessed with the idea of building a new empire for his family in the "Land of Flowers."

The idea of relocating to Florida was the topic of long discussions in the Bellamy and Croom households, the men talking of Hardy's observations while smoking cigars and sipping from fine crystal. Edward's brother, Samuel, had graduated from medical school at the University of Pennsylvania in 1834 and was courting the beautiful young Elizabeth Jane Croom. Like his brother, he fell in love with a place he had never seen – Florida.

Samuel's courtship with Elizabeth was carried out according to the societal customs of the times. Elizabeth's father had died in 1829, so Samuel sought and was granted the permission of her mother to begin the courtship. The young couple danced together at balls and parties in the grand mansions of their neighborhood. They chatted in the parlor under the watchful eyes of Elizabeth's mother. Chaperoned carriage rides were a favorite part of their courtship, as were the evenings when Elizabeth played Samuel favorites on the beautiful parlor piano. The fondness that had existed between the two young people grew to become a deep and abiding love.

As his courtship with Elizabeth went forward, Samuel also worked with his brother in planning their joint relocation south to Florida. Hardy had already explored much of the area between Tallahassee and Pensacola and it was likely at his advice that the brothers focused in on the rich lands along the upper Chipola River. Edward purchased the Fort plantation, where the already old Fort Road crossed the Chipola River at today's Bellamy Bridge site. He and Ann dreamed of life in the country and they soon commissioned the building of a beautiful, columned mansion on a hill overlooking the fields and gently flowing waters of the Chipola.

Samuel and Elizabeth, meanwhile, preferred the culture and social opportunities of life in the city. Although Marianna was still a small town, it was populated by people who were exceptionally wealthy and politically connected. Beautiful homes were rising in the city and it was there that, according to legend, Samuel selected a site within view of the new Jackson County Courthouse for the construction of what was undoubtedly the grandest and most elaborate mansion in the Florida Territory.

Later to be called the Nickels Inn, the Bellamy mansion was a magnificent two story affair that stood upon an entire city block of its own. The floor to ceiling windows allowed for cooling breezes to flow through the house and were paned with glass brought to Apalachicola or St. Joseph by ship and then carefully transported through the wilderness to Marianna. Marble for the fireplace mantels came from Europe. Chandeliers arrived from New York. The finest woods and bricks were selected for use in the construction of the house and its scope and scale would impress those who saw it all the way into the 20th century.

The grounds could only be described as spectacular. There were trees and flowers, formal gardens and a rose garden that bloomed in profusion with every variety then known in the South.

The house and gardens were completed on schedule in May 1837, just as guests from around the country began to arrive in Marianna for Samuel and Elizabeth's wedding. It was, the story tellers say, the "event of the year, if not the decade." Beautiful gifts came from as far away as Europe. Everyone who was anyone from New York to Florida was there.

The wedding itself, the legend holds, took place in the beautiful rose garden that Samuel had planted for his bride. Reciting vows they had written in part themselves, they promised to "love each other, always." It was a touching and beautiful ceremony and it is said that there were few if any dry eyes among those who witnessed it.

The wedding was followed by a magnificent reception in the mansion. There was a string quartet and dancing, tables groaning with the finest foods and wines, fine cigars for the men and roses for the ladies. As evening fell, the mansion blazed with light and the sounds of laughter echoed through the still dirt streets of Marianna, a city that accepted with pride the observation of a visitor that, "In Marianna they drink from a glass, in Webbville from a jug."

Elizabeth and Samuel danced into the evening, surrounded by their guests who enjoyed the celebration immensely. It was an exciting, magical and exhausting affair. Elizabeth, worn down by a day of emotion and excitement, excused herself to the bridal suite on the second floor to rest for a bit and recover her energy.

The legend tells of how she sank down into a deep, cushioned chair, still wearing her beautiful gown. The fireplace blazed low before her, surrounding her with warmth, and a flickering candelabra glowed from a table beside her chair, giving the room a light that was low and warm. Surrounded by luxury, warm and content, the exhausted young bride drifted off into a deep and happy sleep.

Downstairs, the party continued without pause as the guests danced and the men smoked cigars. The reception was still in full swing when the sound of a piercing scream suddenly ripped through the house. All eyes turned to the elegant staircase, shocked to the core by the sight that emerged there.

Elizabeth Jane Bellamy, the beautiful young bride of plantation aristocracy, came shrieking down the stairs. Her body was engulfed in flame from head to foot. Gasps and screams of terror erupted from the guests as Elizabeth ran through the front doors of the mansion, flame and smoke and the smell of burning flash trailing behind her. Samuel and other men rushed to save her, but her pain was so excruciating and her panic so complete that she was difficult to catch. They finally did reach her and push her to the ground, rolling her in the dirt of the street and using their unprotected hands to beat out the flames that flared from her body.

Elizabeth's beautiful gown had somehow come into contact with an open flame. Some say she must have brushed against the candelabra, others that a spark from the open fireplace ignited her dress. She awoke to searing pain and fire that had already engulfed her body. Despite the best efforts of the men to save her life and extinguish the fire, she received the worst burns that Samuel, Edward or any of the other doctors in the crowd had ever seen. How she survived at all was a mystery that none could explain.

The fire-withered body of the once beautiful young woman was carried into the house where doctors did all they could to relieve her pain. Unfortunately, there was little they could do to help. Elizabeth writhed and moaned in pain that was far beyond anything anyone in Marianna had ever experienced. She lingered for perhaps another day. With a voice that was reduced to a hoarse and agonized whisper, she called for Samuel to lean his ear close to her lips. As he did so, with a voice that could barely be heard, she gave to him her dying words, "I will love you… always."

Elizabeth Jane Croom Bellamy, the 18-year-old bride of Dr. Samuel C. Bellamy, was laid to rest on a quiet hill on the plantation of Samuel's brother, Edward. The grave was within sight of Edward and Ann's beautiful home and Samuel knew that it would always be cared for there and that Ann would gently place flowers on the earth that covered the earthly remains of her beloved sister.

Samuel, it is said, descended into alcoholism. He represented Jackson County at the Florida Constitutional Convention in St. Joseph the following year and was one of the men responsible for drafting the constitution that helped secure statehood for Florida. He also served as Clerk of Courts for Jackson County, practiced medicine and was clerk for the Supreme Court of Florida. Alcoholism and depression, however, marked the rest of his life. In one spell he fell so near to insanity that Edward took control of his properties and assets. The two men quarreled over the move and Samuel sued Edward for the return of his property. The case was still underway when Samuel put a razor to his throat and killed himself in the old inn at Chattahoochee Landing on December 28, 1853. He had never remarried.

As the years passed and strife tore apart the once close-knit family, the slaves on Edward Bellamy's plantation began to tell each other of the mysterious woman in white who arose from her grave to walk in the night. She carried with her an unnatural glow and her heart-rending moans struck horror into the hearts of even the bravest men.

Edward Bellamy left Jackson County shortly before the War Between the States, abandoning the beautiful mansion near the wooden bridge that had come to bear his name. The house eventually succumbed to accidental fire, but the old bridge survived. It was replaced and rebuilt several times through the years and eventually replaced with the steel-frame structure that served travelers for much of the 20th century. It survived through the years, a reminder of the optimistic young doctor who had arrived in Jackson County with his beautiful young bride many years before.

The story of Elizabeth's ghost also survived. Stories were told of how she appeared each night, searching for her love who already lay buried in an unmarked grave far away. The ghost story, in fact, grew substantially over the years. The ruins of Edward and Ann's mansion near the bridge came to be associated with the story of the terrible wedding night disaster and some claimed that Elizabeth's spirit could be seen running from the house site to Bellamy Bridge, engulfed in flame that illuminated the night with brilliant light. Others described the ghost as a ball of fire that fell from the sky into the river by the bridge on certain nights when conditions were right.

The beautiful mansion in Marianna survived for many years but eventually fell into disrepair and, like so many of the city's beautiful old homes, was demolished. City Hall stands on the site today.

There are, of course, other variations of the tale, but the basic details are as written above. It is a tragic and romantic story, but is it true? And does Elizabeth Jane Bellamy really haunt the environs of old Bellamy Bridge? The answers to those questions are far more complicated than you might expect.

Chapter Two
Samuel and Elizabeth

Samuel and Elizabeth Bellamy were real people and, while the true story of their lives differs significantly from the legend, it is just as poignant and just as tragic.

Samuel C. Bellamy was born into a wealthy North Carolina family in 1810. After receiving a solid education in private schools, he went on to attend the highly regarded medical school at the University of Pennsylvania, where he was listed in the graduating class of 1834. A properly educated gentleman of his day, Samuel could recite the classics; speak and read in Latin, Greek, French and possibly even German; discuss the latest political issues, and manage the affairs of a large plantation. His medical training gave him an understanding of anatomy, chemical compounds and then accepted treatments for a number of ailments and injuries.

It was an strange time in America. While most people of the day were not wealthy, young aristocrats like Bellamy pursued higher interests and courted the young women of their dreams, even as enslaved Africans sweated and performed backbreaking labors in the fields and workshops. The lives of the wealthy elite were not the norm for the time or for the South. Most white and free black Southerners of the 1830s worked on small farms or as craftsmen and the percentage of the Southern population that owned slaves was very small. In modern terms, aristocrats like the brothers Samuel, Edward and Alexander Bellamy were the wealthiest of the wealthy, people we see rarely see today except on television or in magazines.

Elizabeth Jane Croom, Samuel's young bride, was also the child of such a family. Her father, Major General William Croom, had commanded North Carolina troops during the War of 1812 and owned multiple plantations around Kinston in Lenoir County. The younger sister of Ann, Bryan and Hardy Bryan Croom, she was born in 1819.

Only ten years old when her father died in 1829, Elizabeth was left extensive holdings in land, slaves and other wealth. Although she is often called "Betsy" by tellers of the ghost story, she was identified in her father's will by the nickname "Eliza." Her sister Ann married Dr. Edward C. Bellamy in December of that same year. The couple undoubtedly maintained close ties to young Elizabeth, and as a teenager she became enamored of Edward's brother, Samuel, who was a young man eight years her senior.

Both the Croom and Bellamy families were part of a wave of wealthy planters from North Carolina that flooded into Florida during the 1820s. The prime cotton lands of the Tar Heel State were diminishing in quality due to overuse, but Florida plantations and farms were reporting record crops. Elizabeth's father, General William Croom, first visited Florida in 1826 to explore the area of Leon, Gadsden and Jackson Counties. The general's second wife was Mary Bryan and members of her family settled in and around the Jackson County town of Greenwood during the 1820s. Undoubtedly, the various families interested in making the migration were discussing and reporting conditions with each other.

General Croom returned to Florida in 1828 and purchased extensive properties in Gadsden County. His son, Bryan, went down with an overseer and some of the family's slaves to open land and begin planting. The general planned to return to Florida the following year, but died in misery from a "bilious fever" on May 9, 1829, the very day he had planned to begin his next journey south.

The general's death was the first in a series of tragic events that would strike the Croom and Bellamy families over the next two years. Although the families could not have known it at the time, the magnitude of these disasters is stunning today even after the passage of nearly two centuries of time.

Despite the death of his father, Hardy Bryan Croom returned to Florida in 1829 and with his brother, Bryan, purchased additional lands in Gadsden, Jackson and eventually Leon Counties. Among these properties was a parcel of over 400 acres in Jackson County that the brothers called their "river plantation." It was located on the west side of the Apalachicola River south of the modern community of Sneads, about where Interstate 10 now crosses the river.

At about the same time, and possibly as part of the same immigrating party, Alexander A. Bellamy arrived in Florida. It is not known whether he explored the area at an earlier date, but he first appears on county records in Jackson County in 1829 and the census of the following year shows him living there with his wife, Sarah Boykin, children and 15 slaves.

Alexander was the older brother of Drs. Samuel C. Bellamy and Edward C. Bellamy. He was born in 1788, one year before the signing of the U.S. Constitution. The middle brother, Edward, married Ann Croom on December 17, 1829. The oldest of General William Croom's daughters, she was the sister of Elizabeth, Bryan and Hardy Bryan. Edward was 28 at the time and she was 17.

Much of the migration of the Bellamy and Croom families to Florida was encouraged and supervised by Hardy Bryan Croom. Well educated and a noted botanist of the day, Hardy Bryan maintained his residence in North Carolina and even served in the state senate there, all the while spending more and more time in Florida and buying more and more property. The Gadsden County farms were devoted primarily to cotton production, while the "river plantation" in Jackson County was a sugar plantation. It is seldom remembered today that many investors of the 1820s expected Florida was to rival Cuba in the production of sugar. It never happened, but heavy investments were made in sugarcane farms by some of the earliest settlers.

Hardy Bryan Croom's "river plantation" was on the west side of the Apalachicola River at about the point it is now crossed by Interstate 10:

It was in passing from this plantation to the one near Quincy that he discovered one of the rarest of coniferous trees, which he named Toreya taxifolium. There are four species of this tree, of remarkable distribution, according to the "New International Encyclopedia," second edition. All the species are very local and very widely separated, occurring in restricted localities in China, Japan, California and Florida. After Mr. Croom ascertained that it was the first discovered in the United States of this species of coniferous tree, he desired that it should bear the name of Dr. John Torrey, a famous botanist of that time living in the city of New York, with whom he had collaborated in botanical work. Mr. Croom also discovered in Florida the botanically curious little plant which Dr. Torrey named Croomia panciflora in his honor.[1]

The Florida Torreya , discovered by Hardy Bryan Croom, is one of the rarest trees in the world and its last surviving stands are preserved at Torreya State Park and the adjacent Apalachicola Bluffs & Ravines Preserve in Liberty County. An old Florida legend holds that this region was the site of the Biblical Garden of Eden and that the Torreya was the "gopher wood" from which Noah built the ark.[1]

Hardy Croom's influence on both the Croom and Bellamy families was strong. It has already been noted that Alexander A. Bellamy arrived in Jackson County with his family and slaves in 1829. Hardy, meanwhile, continued to correspond with others in the two families about the potential wealth to be gained by settling early in Florida and claiming the best lands. Among those with whom he discussed such prospects was his brother-in-law, Dr. Edward C. Bellamy. There was some resistance to the idea among the women of the families, but the men succumbed quickly to the "Florida fever."

Alexander Bellamy undoubtedly also exerted an influence on his younger brothers. Having established himself in Jackson County, he returned home to North Carolina and married Sarah Boykin on December 29, 1829, roughly two weeks after Edward Bellamy married Ann Croom. Undoubtedly there was much discussion about Florida at both events. Alexander continued to correspond with Edward about the prospects of moving the family's entire operations to Florida. By the time they returned to North Carolina in July 1834 for Samuel Bellamy's wedding to Elizabeth Jane Croom, Alexander and Sarah had started a family that included a little girl and twin boys.

The third of the Bellamy brothers, Samuel, graduated from medical school at the University of Pennsylvania in June 1834. He had been courting Elizabeth Jane Croom long distance and it is at this point that the true story of the couple begins to separate itself from the legend.

Family correspondence, marriage records and newspaper archives indicate conclusively that Samuel and Elizabeth were married in Lenoir County, North Carolina, on July 15, 1834. This was three years before the supposed Florida wedding and accidental fire. Samuel was 24 years old and Elizabeth was 15, reasonable ages for the time, and they began their life together with every possible prospect of a bright future. Both were the children of elite North Carolina families and both possessed considerable independent wealth. The wedding did not take place in Marianna, as legend holds, but at Newington Plantation near Kinston, North Carolina. And Elizabeth did not die on her wedding night, but continued to live with her husband in North Carolina for nearly another two years.

---

[1] To learn more about the Garden of Eden legend, please see *Two Egg, Florida: A Collection of Ghost Stories, Legends & Unusual Facts*, by this author.

Alexander and Sarah, meanwhile, returned home to Jackson County after Samuel and Elizabeth's wedding and resumed the management of their home and plantation. Tragedy, however, was stalking on the heels of the Bellamy and Croom families. It soon reared its head in the form of fever, the monstrous malady that claimed thousands of lives in the Deep South during the antebellum era.

An outbreak of fever (probably malaria) exploded across the Florida Panhandle in the late fall of 1834. The sickness did not respect age, sex or status, but instead brought down people from all walks of life. Anna Maria Beveridge, one of the women for whom Marianna was named, had already died from fever and in 1834 many other Jackson County residents followed. Alexander A. Bellamy and his young daughter were among them.

The unfortunate man was suffering from fever and in extremely poor health on December 17, 1834, when he completed his last will and testament. He clearly had a premonition of his death, for he requested that his body be carried home to North Carolina and buried in the family cemetery. He died before the end of the month, as did his little girl. Whether he was carried home for burial is not known.

Ironically, it was not long after Alexander's death that his two brothers, Edward and Samuel, decided to make preparations for a relocation of their families to Florida. Hardy Bryan Croom had resigned his seat in the North Carolina State Senate and taken up residence at Goodwood Plantation near Tallahassee. Bryan Croom was well established at Rocky Comfort in Gadsden County and two of the Croom sisters, Ann and Elizabeth, now prepared to join their siblings in Florida.

Elizabeth gave birth to a little boy in December 1835 and she and Samuel named him Alexander in honor of his lost brother. By the time the baby was born, the two sisters and their families had agreed to move to Florida. Edward and Ann acquired a plantation on the Chipola River north of Marianna that included the land on both sides of the river where Bellamy Bridge stands today. Samuel and Elizabeth, meanwhile, purchased a large tract on Baker Creek about three miles northwest of Marianna. Not far from the little town of Webbville, the plantation surrounded Jackson County's well-known Rock Arch Cave, which is today known as the Gerrard's or Sam Smith Cave. The presence of this beautiful natural feature inspired the name of the farm, "Rock Cave Plantation."

The movement of the two families and their holdings to Florida was a massive undertaking that began in early 1836. In addition to Elizabeth and Samuel, Ann and Edward, and their children, the move included an overseer naed R.B. Carlton and more than 100 African slaves. It was also necessary to move everything needed to operate the new plantations as well as household furniture, kitchen utensils, personal possessions and more. The wagon trains must have stretched for as far as the eye could see and the journey must have been incredibly difficult in that day before modern roads and conveniences.

Samuel and Elizabeth's overseer, R.B. Carlton, later testified about his arrival and work for the couple in Jackson County:

...[H]e came to this country with Samuel Bellamy, and overseered for him in the years 1836, 1837, 1839 and 1840, that he was well acquainted with the character and value of Samuel C. Bellamy's negroes, and that there were 40 working hands at the time he overseered for him, and were as valuable a set of hands as any in Jackson County. That he settled the plantation, and cleared most of the land; that there were a good many likely young hands growing up at the time. The land was very good, and Samuel C. Bellamy once in his presence, refused $20 per acre; and witness considers it would make as much per acre as any land in the country, and that he has made it.[2]

The place to which the two families came was immensely beautiful. Rock Cave Plantation, where Samuel and Elizabeth settled as their slaves worked to clear fields and plant subsistence crops to feed the people of the self-sustaining farm, was a place of streams, caves and rolling hills. Rt. Rev. Michael Portier, a Catholic bishop, passed through the vicinity about nine years before the Bellamy family arrived:

...On every side you could hear the rippling of the brooks which here and there blended the waters and developed into streams of deep and regular formation. Rocks were to be met as high as the trees themselves, and bordered around with wild flowers, while sweet-scented shrubbery decked the sides and summits of these pygmy mountains. Natural wells, underground caves, oak trees blasted by lightning or cast by the tempest across our narrow pathway like an artificial bridge – everything was present to enhance the spectacle.[3]

The magnificent Rock Arch or Rock Cave, from which the plantation drew its name, was already something of a tourist attraction by the time Samuel and Elizabeth arrived in Florida. There can be little doubt that the young couple explored its beautiful chambers in person:

...After a moderate descent of about twenty feet, it opens into a spacious hall of white lime-stone, about 180 feet in length, by 100 in breadth, and from 20 to 30 feet high. The top is a regular arch, supported by two pillars, which appear to have been formed by the dripping of water from the top of the cave. These pillars appear like fluted columns, with a base and capital of curious carved work. The dripping of water from the top of the cave, has also formed stalactites, which are suspended from the roof like icicles from the roof of the house. On the floor of the cave are numerous bodies, formed also by the dripping of water, of a variety of shapes, some resembling benches, tables, &c.; and others the heads and bodies of animals, and all appearing like the most beautiful carved work.[4]

Whether Samuel and Elizabeth knew it is not known, but the cave held a romantic history that went back more than 150 years. There is reason to believe it was the site of Mission San Nicolas, where Fray Rodrigo de la Barreda came to preach the Gospel to the people of the Chacato tribe back in 1674:

Here we spent the night in the hollow of such a beautiful and unusual rock that I can state positively that more than 200 men could be lodged most comfortably within it; inside there is a brook which gushes from the living rock. It has plenty of light and height with three apertures buttressed by stonework of unusual natural architecture. Around it are level plots of ground, groves of trees and pine woods, all of which are delightful....[5]

Andrew Jackson also visited the cave, about 18 years before Samuel and Elizabeth arrived to farm the rich lands that surrounded it. His topographer, Captain Hugh Young, described it in less than romantic terms as a large cave inside which a spring of water flowed, but wrote admiringly of the beauty and richness of the surrounding lands.

The lands of Rock Cave Plantation were indeed beautiful and rich, but they were also deadly. The swamps of Baker Creek and the Chipola River were breeding grounds for mosquitoes and fevers and chills were common enemies of early settlers, black and white alike. The Bellamy family was not spared.

On December 6, 1836, Hardy Bryan Croom wrote to his wife that Samuel, Elizabeth and baby Alexander were all sick with a fever that must have been malaria. Sometimes called the "intermittent and remittent fever" by doctors of the time because patients often recovered only to suddenly collapse and often die in vicious relapses of the illness, malaria – along with its cousin, yellow fever – was far deadlier to the early settlers of Florida than Seminole attacks and any of the other disasters that often befell families in the new territory.[6]

It was fever and not fire that claimed the life of the beautiful young woman named Elizabeth Jane Bellamy on May 11, 1837. Her 18-month old son, baby Alexander, died seven days later on the 18th.[7]

That Elizabeth Bellamy died of fever in her bed and not of a tragic wedding night fire is indisputable. Her obituary appeared in the Tallahassee *Floridian* and other newspapers of the time and her passing was mentioned in the letters of both Samuel C. Bellamy and Hardy Bryan Croom. She was laid to rest not at Rock Cave, but at the plantation of Edward and Ann Bellamy where Bellamy Bridge stands today. Baby Alexander was buried beside her.

The decision to bury her there probably was made so that her sister, Ann, could watch over her grave. The little cemetery was within view of she and Edward had built.

The death of his 18-year-old wife and 18-month-old child devastated Samuel Bellamy. Legend is correct in its assertion that he descended into the pits of alcoholic despair. The transition from prosperous young planter to depressed alcoholic, however, did not take place immediately.

Determined to make a life for himself in Florida despite the loss of Elizabeth and the baby, he accepted a position as the Marianna appraiser for the Union Bank of Florida. Bank records show that Samuel was awarded 148 shares worth $14,800 on February 10, 1838, for use in building a new home. The awarding of shares was the way the Union Bank loaned money. Land owners mortgaged their property to secure the value of the shares they were awarded and then used the money for the purpose for which they needed financing.

Based on the value of currency in 1838, $14,800 was an impressive sum. The money, of course, was used to build Samuel's magnificent mansion in Marianna. It was not a wedding gift for his blushing young bridge, but instead was financed and built roughly one year after her death.

Samuel's status in the community was also reflected by his selection to be one of Jackson County's four delegates to the Florida Constitutional Convention of 1838. He served on the convention's banking committee and took an active part in drafting Florida's original constitution. He also addressed the assembled delegates on the importance of the work entrusted to them:

...Many of us...are not politicians by profession; we do not look to politics as an object from whence to derive support for our families, we take no delight in party strife or political turmoil – but have come here with another view, and are influenced by no other motives, than to discharge honestly the trust committed to us by our constituents, and to lay the foundation of the government, which we humbly hope is to advance the future prosperity and happiness of the good people of Florida.[8]

His participation in the Constitutional Convention of 1838 as a respected planter and bank appraiser was perhaps the high point of Dr. Samuel Bellemy's life in Florida. Tragedy and misfortune continued to stalk him with a persistence that must have been overwhelming. The series of events and family disasters that began with the deaths of Elizabeth and Alexander had continued on October 9, 1837, when Hardy Bryan Croom, his wife and their three children died in the steamship *Home* disaster on the Outer Banks of North Carolina. Within six months, seven members of the Croom and Bellamy families suffered tragic deaths.

Samuel Bellamy had come to Florida expecting to live the life of a prosperous planter and gentlemen. Despite the tragedies that befell his family, he tried to continue forward with the realization of his dreams.. He returned home from the Constitutional Convention in St. Joseph to live in his beautiful mansion, continue his work for the Union Bank and tend to the operation of Rock Cave Plantation. In these pursuits he was initially successful. Rock Cave prospered. The long staple cotton grown there was widely praised for its quality and old Apalachicola newspapers note with some degree of regularity the arrival of barges loaded with Bellamy cotton.

Like other planters along the Chipola River, Samuel sent much of his cotton crop down the narrow stream on wooden barges. Sturdy, shallow-draft vessels capable of carrying heavy cargoes, these barges exited the mouth of the Chipola into the Apalachicola River and eventually floated on down to either Apalachicola or St. Joseph. Paddlewheel steamboats were usually used to tow them once they reached the big river. Some farmers hauled their cotton bales by ox cart to landings on the Chattahoochee and Apalachicola Rivers, but so far as is known, all of Samuel's went down the Chipola.

Ocean-going schooners and sloops provided transport from the port cities of Apalachicola and St. Joseph on to the markets of New England. The two cities spent the late 1830s waging commercial war against each other. Apalachicola was the older of the two and its position at the mouth of the river gave it a natural advantage. St. Joseph hoped to divert traffic away from its nearby competitor, however, by building a railroad that would allow paddlewheel steamboats to shorten their voyage by offloading their cargoes to the trains for a quick trip over to St. Joseph Bay.

By the time Samuel Bellamy attended the Florida Constitutional Convention in St. Joseph in 1838, the city was home to nearly 12,000 residents and had emerged as the largest municipality in the territory. Many of its key investors financed their homes and businesses by borrowing heavily on their plantations and properties in the interior. Much of this borrowing was done through the Union Bank, of which Samuel was an appraiser. In 1840, however, just three years after Elizabeth's death, things started to go badly wrong. The national economy began to fail and cotton prices experienced an unexpected drop. A yellow fever outbreak virtually depopulated St. Joseph in 1841, killing its citizens – including Marianna's founder Robert Beveridge – by the dozens. The city would never recover.

By the time a massive hurricane hit in 1844, St. Joseph was all but gone. Houses had been dismantled and moved to nearby Apalachicola and those that survived were either destroyed by the storm or allowed to deteriorate. In less than five years, Florida's largest city had disappeared from the map.

It was a disastrous blow that was too much for the economy of the territory to absorb. The Union Bank failed in 1843 and Congressional investigators later determined that its officers had engaged in extravagance and that it had loaned money in amounts far exceeding its resources. Investors in the bank lost fortunes.

Among those who owed the bank far more than the values of their lands was Samuel Bellamy. He was indebted for $27,710 by the time the bank closed its doors. His fortune was gone. He began to practice medicine and undertook bridge construction projects for the county as a way of making ends meet, but lawsuits piled up against him.

One of the bridge building projects contracted to Bellamy by Jackson County was for a strong wooden bridge across the Chipola River near Marianna. While it has long been thought that this was the first wooden structure at today's Bellamy Bridge site, this may not have been the case. There was, of course, much need for a bridge at Edward and Ann Bellamy's Terre Bonne Plantation, but it appears more likely that the bridge contracted to Samuel in 1844 was actually at Marianna itself. Samuel seems to have started the project in good faith, but his creditors were by then pressing down on him and he was on the verge of losing everything.

It was at this moment that he and Edward struck an agreement by which Samuel thought he might be able to save his estate. For the sum of $1.00, he transferred ownership of Rock Cave Plantation to Edward, apparently as a way of protecting it from being seized. The agreement was signed on November 19, 1844, and included all of Samuel's lands, livestock, improvements, slaves and "his right and interest in and to the contract for constructing the bridge across the Chipola river near Marianna."[9]

The contract went on to specify, however, that Samuel could continue to enjoy his holdings and bridge contract:

Nevertheless, upon this especial trust and confidence herein and hereby created and declared, to wit: that the aforesaid Edward Bellamy shall have and hold the aforesaid property upon the following stated trust and for these interests, objects and purposes, hereinafter set forth, that is to say, that the said Samuel C. Bellamy shall continue and remain in possession of all this property and effects above specified, and shall proceed with his contract in relation to the bridge, that the said Edward C. Bellamy shall receive all the rents, profits, hire and income, derived from the same....[10]

The bridge referred to in the agreement between the two brothers was completed by Samuel sometime during the winter of 1844-1845, about six years before the Jackson County Board of County Commissioners began to seriously consider a structure at today's Bellamy Bridge site.

Despite the desperate measure to keep Samuel's holdings under family control, things continued to deteriorate for him. He turned more and more to alcohol as a remedy for his troubles and soon found himself battling severe alcoholism and depression. Things got worse as Edward exerted more and more control over Samuel's former properties, leaving him with little or nothing upon which to live. By 1848, Samuel was running ads in the *Florida Whig* newspaper in Marianna, appealing to his friends to support his medical practice as he had no other means of supporting himself due to what he considered the wrongdoing committed against him by his brother.

He tried to battle alcoholism by joining the Chipola Division of the Sons of Temperance and on July 4, 1849, addressed a large crowd in Marianna about the evils of alcohol. "The cup is offered," he said. "He seizes it with the avidity a drowning man would catch at a straw, and buries alike his sorrows and his senses in oblivion." His battle for sobriety, however, would fail.

Despite his well-known battle with liquor, Samuel served as Clerk of Courts for Jackson County and in 1852 was named deputy clerk of the Supreme Court of Florida. On December 28, 1853, sixteen years after the death of his wife and child, Dr. Samuel C. Bellamy cut his own throat with a straight razor in a tavern and inn at Chattahoochee Landing. Dr. Charles Hentz, a prominent local physician, noted that Samuel was "laboring under delirium tremens" at the time of his death and had been "exceedingly intemperate for years past."[11]

Samuel Bellamy was only 44 years old when he took his own life. In a final, sad footnote to his life, he left instructions in his will for his executor to "prosecute to the limit of the law against Edward C. Bellamy, until he shall be compelled to account for and pay over the last cent he has of mine." Samuel's estate eventually did prevail against Edward, but most of the assets were seized to satisfy the debts owed the Union Bank.

Edward and Ann continued to live in Jackson County for a time, but left Florida for Mississippi shortly before the beginning of the War Between the States. Their house near Bellamy Bridge was eventually destroyed in an accidental fire and today nothing remains but a barely discernible cistern to indicate the grand mansion ever stood at all. Elizabeth's grave likewise has been lost to the public and is now on private property and no longer accessible. So far as is known, Samuel rests in an unmarked grave in Chattahoochee.

---

[1] Florida Law Journal, Volume IX, May 1935, No.5.

[2] Testimony of R.B. Carlton in Edward C. Bellamy vs. the Sheriff of Jackson County; Florida Supreme Court Term of 1855, Tallahassee, Florida; Mario D. Papy, Reporter, *Cases Argued and Adjudged in the Supreme Court of Florida at Terms Held in 1855*, Volume VI, No. 1, Tallahassee, Office of the Florida Sentinel, Printed by Benj. F. Allen, 1855, pp. 85-86.

[3] Rt. Rev. Michael Portier, "From Pensacola to St. Augustine in 1827: A Journey of the Rt. Rev. Michael Portier," *Florida Historical Quarterly*, Volume 26, Issue 2, p. 150.

[4] *Providence Patriot*, October 23, 1823, p. 2,

[5] Fray Rodrigo de la Barreda, "Journal," 1693 (copy in private collection of author).

[6] Hardy Bryan Croom to Wife, December 6, 1836, Croom Family Papers, University of North Carolina.

[7] Tallahassee *Floridian*, May 1837.

[8] Tallahassee *Floridian*, December 1838.

[9] Indenture between Samuel C. Bellamy and Edward C. Bellamy, November 19, 1844.

[10] *Ibid.*

[11] Dale Cox, *The History of Jackson County, Florida: The Early Years,* (Volume One), Bascom, Florida, 2008, pp. 227-229.

Chapter Three

The Real "Burning Bride"

It is easy to understand how the tragic lives of Elizabeth and Samuel Bellamy could have given rise to a multitude of ghost stories, but comprehending how their story could have evolved into the tale of the "burning bride of Bellamy Bridge" is a bit more difficult. The answer to the mystery lies in the writings of a 19th century novelist perhaps best known as the author of the Southern rebuttal to Harriett Beecher Stowe's *Uncle Tom's Cabin*.

Caroline Lee Hentz was a prolific author much loved in her day for a noteworthy series of romantic novels. With her husband, Nicholas, she traveled from city to city across much of the eastern United States, living at times in North Carolina, Ohio, Alabama, Georgia and finally Florida. She had been a member of the same literary guild as Stowe, but took great exception to the portrayal of slavery and the South as given in *Uncle Tom's Cabin*. In her rebuttal, titled *Planter's Northern Bride*, she tried to give the view of the Southern elite and their slaves about the matter. It was, of course, a much romanticized view, but to her credit Mrs. Hentz was quick to recognize the intellectual and artistic abilities of individual African Americans. She once played an important role, for example, in the development and literary education of a talented African American poet and actively attempted to secure his freedom from slavery.

In 1853, three years before she died in Marianna, Mrs. Hentz published a fascinating little volume that she titled *Marcus Warland or the Long Moss Spring*. The title and the fact that she spent much of the final two years of her life in Marianna or in a summer cottage at St. Andrew Bay led many in later years to assume that the book was written in and about Jackson County. The "long moss spring" of the title, in fact, is still widely believed to have been Blue Springs near Marianna, although in fact the association is incorrect.

In reality, Caroline Hentz wrote *Marcus Warland* while she was living in Columbus, Georgia, prior to relocating to Florida. It was based largely on the people and places she observed in that area and is unique because of the detail it gives to daily events in a plantation slave community. The book also provides a detailed account of the death of a young woman named Cora who, having exhausted herself dancing on her wedding night, went upstairs to rest briefly before rejoining the party:

...Turning away she threw herself into a large easy-chair in front of the fire, and in spite of the excited state of her feelings and the extreme want of sentiment evinced by the act, she fell asleep in her downy next. She had been up almost all the preceding night, on her feet all day, and had been dancing with such extraordinary enthusiasm, that the soft cushion and gentle warmth of the room soother her to instantaneous repose. How long she slept, she knew not. She was awakened by a sense of heat and suffocation, as if her lungs were turned to fire. Starting up she found herself encircled by a blaze of light that seemed to emanate from her own body. Her light dress was one sheet of flame, the chair she left was enveloped in the same destroying element.[1]

The young bride who found herself in such tragic circumstances on her wedding night was not the darling child of antebellum aristocracy, but instead was a young slave woman. Her mistress, Mrs. Hentz wrote, was so attached to Cora that she arranged for her wedding to take place in the main house and provided her with the finest of everything, including a magnificent wedding gown. The name chosen by the novelist for the mistress of the plantation, as you probably have guessed, was "Mrs. Bellamy."

The story continues almost like a word for word recitation of the Bellamy Bridge legend:

...Mrs. Bellamy, who was in the room below, heard the sudden terrible cry of human suffering, and flew to relieve it. When she beheld the blazing figure leaping towards the open door, and recognized the voice of Cora, shrill and piercing as it now was, regardless of self, she sprang after her, and seizing her with frenzied grasp, tried to crush the flames with her slender fingers, and smother them against her own body. While she was thus heroically endeavouring to save the

beautiful mulatto at the risk of her own life, Hannibal, who had dragged the carpet from the hall, wrapped it closely around the form of her he so madly loved....[2]

Hannibal, another slave, was the man Cora had passed over when she agreed to marry her groom, whose name was King. The young woman lingered several days before she finally died from the horrible burns she had received. The fire had been caused when her wedding gown came into contact with a candle burning near her chair.

Cora, Mrs. Hentz went on to relate, was buried in a small cemetery on the "Bellamy plantation," where her grave was surrounded by flowers and shrubs:

...The mourning bridegroom of an hour planted a weeping-willow by its side, and many a night, when the moon was shining on her grave, the tall, dark form of Hannibal would wander to the spot, certain that he met there the spirit of Cora, and that she looked kindly upon him. Indeed, all the negroes on the plantation saw her ghost, and it was always dressed like a bride, in white muslin, white roses, and white kid gloves.[3]

Because Caroline Hentz moved to Marianna not long after the publication of *Marcus Warland* and died in the city just a few years later, the story of the unfortunate young woman who was severely burned on her wedding night on the "Bellamy plantation" came to be associated with the lonely grave of Elizabeth Jane Bellamy near Bellamy Bridge. The two stories, in short, became one, with the real tragedy of Elizabeth's life being replaced by the horrible death of the "burning bride" in Mrs. Hentz's novel.

The coincidence is rendered even more remarkable by the fact that "Cora" of *Marcus Warland* was a real person. In her "Address to the Reader" at the beginning of the book, Mrs. Hentz wrote as follows:

The description of Mr. Bellamy's plantation is drawn from the real, not the ideal. The incident recorded of Mrs. Bellamy, of her endeavouring to rescue the mulatto girl from the flames at the risk of her own life, occurred during the last winter in our city. The lady who really performed the heroic and self-serving deed is a friend of our own, and we saw her when her scarred and bandaged hands bore witness to her humanity and sufferings.[4]

The introductory explanation was datelined from Columbus, Georgia. Attempts to learn the real identity of "Mrs. Bellamy" and more detail about the actual death of "Cora" have been met with frustration. The newspapers of Columbus seem not to have taken note of the death of a young slave woman, even under such tragic circumstances.

Caroline Hentz died in Marianna in 1856 and is buried in the small cemetery at St. Luke's Episcopal Church. Her memory has largely faded from the modern generation, but her heartbreaking story of the death of a young slave named Cora lives on in the legend of the "Burning Bride" of Bellamy Bridge.

---

[1] Carolina Lee Hentz, *Marcus Warland or the Long Moss Spring*, 1853.
[2] *Ibid.*
[3] *Ibid.*
[4] *Ibid.*

Chapter Four

The Ghosts of Bellamy Bridge

The unveiling of the true facts about Samuel and Elizabeth Bellamy in no way disproves or proves that there is a ghost at Bellamy Bridge. If anything, the real story of their lives is even more tragic than the legend and could easily have spawned a ghost story without the tragic drama of the "burning bride" part of the tale.

The oldest versions of the Bellamy Bridge ghost story, in fact, do not refer to Elizabeth appearing engulfed in flames, but instead as a solitary figure that moved quietly through the trees in the vicinity of the bridge on foggy or stormy nights. The first known reference to a ghost at the bridge appeared in a Marianna newspaper in 1890. Only a single sentence in length, it merely noted that, "The lady of Bellamy Bridge has been seen of late."

The brief mention is fascinating for several reasons. First, it shows that the story was so well-known by 1890 that the editor had only to mention "the lady of Bellamy Bridge" for local readers to understand implicitly that he was referring to the ghost. Second, the ghost was referred to only as "the lady," not as a burning specter. Finally, the association of the ghost with Bellamy Bridge was clear by that point. The newspaper mention, set into type only 53 years after Elizabeth's death, appeared on a date much closer to her lifetime than to our own.

Several senior citizens of Marianna interviewed during the 1980s told similar versions of the ghost story. Slade West, local historian and long-time owner of the historic Davis-West House, indicated that he had always been told the ghost appeared in the form of a young woman. Although he never saw her himself, West said he had heard since childhood that she always appeared dressed in white and could be seen moving in silence through the trees of the swamp near Bellamy Bridge.

Mrs. Bruce Milton Singletary, great-granddaughter of Governor John Milton, also had always heard the ghost described as a young woman dressed all in white. She indicated, however, that eyewitnesses had told her that the ghost could be heard sobbing as it moved through the trees around the bridge.

John Winslett, long-time Marianna journalist and print shop owner, said that he had often heard accounts of the ghost at Bellamy Bridge and thought that the "burning bride" version of the story first became popular at around the time of World War II. Prior to the 1940s, he could only recall having heard that the ghost of a young woman could be seen in the vicinity of the bridge. He also remembered that for the first half of the 20th century, the area immediately around Bellamy Bridge was regarded as something of a dark and foreboding place. Several murders had taken place near the bridge and the narrow, unlit road leading to and from the structure was shrouded by gigantic oak trees.

These accounts are intriguing because they all confirm that the presence of a ghost at Bellamy Bridge was well-known in the community prior to the rise of the burning bride story. It seems to have been during the 1940s that it became widely believed that the 19th century books of Caroline Lee Hentz had been written in and about Jackson County. Few people by that time remembered the exact details of the wedding night fire incident described in *Marcus Warland*, but they did recall its association with the name Bellamy and logically associated it with the lonely grave of Elizabeth Jane Bellamy near Bellamy Bridge. Since a ghost story already existed there, it was easy for the "burning bride" of literature to become joined with the legend.

From the 1940s through the present, the story of the ghost grew in the telling. From the sad and somber figure of a young woman, the specter evolved into a fiery figure that ran out onto the bridge at midnight and, screaming in agony, leaped from its wooden floor into the river below. Another version told of a ball of fire that fell through the framework of the old bridge and was extinguished by the dark waters of the Chipola.

While such lurid tales depart greatly from the early stories of a lonely woman in white, they are part of the cultural progression of the Bellamy Bridge story and as such are important aspects of the legend. What is especially curious, however, is that through the years even as such wild stories were being told, there was an undercurrent of sightings by reliable eyewitnesses of something strange at Bellamy Bridge.

More than fifty eyewitnesses have described seeing mysterious lights at and near Bellamy Bridge. In late October 2012, in fact, a group of twenty-five participants in a guided tour of the new Bellamy Bridge Heritage Trail was stunned by the unexpected appearance of a faint blue light at about the mid-point of the steel-frame structure of the historic bridge. A number of these witnesses were able to obtain photographs of the strange phenomenon, which was seen by the entire group and lasted 7 or 8 seconds before fading away. No reasonable explanation of what it could have been has been forthcoming.

Even more unexpectedly, the mysterious light appeared to a second group of tour participants on the following night. Its appearance this time was of much shorter duration and lasted only 1 or 2 seconds. The sighting took place later in the evening and at a slightly different location near the west end of the bridge. Once again, no reasonable explanation has been offered.

While these mass sightings were particularly unique, reports of blue lights at Bellamy Bridge are far from uncommon. One eyewitness described seeing a bright blue light appear near the bridge in the fall of 1970, while another reported observing such a phenomenon on the west bank of the Chipola just south of the bridge during the mid-1960s. Similar stories abound. Whether they are supernatural or natural phenomena cannot be said, although it should be noted that these lights are very different in appearance from the faint and flickering glow of foxfire that sometimes appears in the adjacent swamp.

It is worth noting that not all of the claims of ghostly activity at and near Bellamy Bridge are associated with the sad story of Elizabeth Jane Bellamy. In fact, some believe that at least three other ghosts haunt the vicinity.

Interviewed for this project in 2011, a former resident of Bellamy Bridge Road told the story of a mysterious figure that could be seen going and coming from the bridge nightly in a mule-drawn wagon. On his way west down the old road to the bridge the man driving the wagon appeared fully human, but on his way back he was said to be missing his head.

The witness indicated that he and his siblings were told this story in childhood by their parents, who warned that if they were not in bed by the appointed time, the man in the wagon would take them to Bellamy Bridge and take away their heads. It is a macabre bedtime story to be sure, but such tales were often told to Southern children in the 19th century and sometimes carried over into the 20th.

A variation of the same legend appears to have been preserved in other Jackson County families as well. Several individuals interviewed to collect their memories of Bellamy Bridge in the 1950s and 1960s recalled having been told that a ghostly wagon sometimes could be heard approaching and crossing the bridge on dark and moonless nights. It was said to be driven by the disturbed spirit of a man who rode on the bench of his wagon across the bridge, illuminated only by the light of a dim lantern.

These stories appear to be associated with a brutal murder/suicide about which only the vaguest details are known. Evidently during the early years of the 20th century, a resident of northern Jackson County became involved in a bitter dispute with his wife. He placed his young daughter on the seat of his wagon and carried her down to a spot near Bellamy Bridge where he decapitated her with an ax before using the blade of the same tool to cut his own throat. Their bodies were found by passersby and carried away for burial. If a coroner's jury held an inquest, the records no longer exist.

Some believe, however, that the ghosts of the man and his unfortunate child still haunt Bellamy Bridge Road and the old bridge itself and are responsible for some of the mysterious lights seen there. The link between the real event and the stories of a haunted wagon are obvious.

A second story of violent murder involves not the current Bellamy Bridge, but the wooden structure that preceded it. Authorized in 1872 to replace a Civil War era span that had been swept away by flooding, this bridge stood at the same spot as today's steel-frame structure. 1914 was the final year of the old wooden bridge's existence and it was in that same year that a moonshining-related murder there shocked the citizens of Jackson County and gave rise to yet another ghost story at Bellamy Bridge.

The Eighteenth Amendment prohibiting the manufacture, sale and transport of liquor in the United States would not be ratified for another five years, but the operation of illegal whiskey stills was already thriving in Jackson County. Moonshiners of that day profited by making cheap liquor and avoiding the taxes levied on the production and sale of alcohol. As is always the case with such illegal enterprises, however, violence and white lightning often went hand in hand.

On May 9, 1914, a dispute broke out in northern Jackson County between three men who were involved in making and selling illegal whiskey and beer. Levi Hart was a storekeeper, but also was involved in moonshining with two of his cousins, Sylvester Hart and Dan Smith. Sylvester was Levi's paternal cousin, while Dan was from his mother's family.

On the day in question the trio discovered that 12 quarts of white lightning was missing and that 5 barrels of homemade beer had been dumped onto the ground. Dan Smith in particular was furious about the loss of so much valuable liquid. He and Levi were convinced that Sylvester had stolen the moonshine to sell for his own profit and that he had also destroyed their jointly owned beer supply.

Even in the court records there is a lot of confusion about what exactly happened that day. After an initial meeting at Levi's store, the three rode out in a buggy together and wound up on Bump Nose Road north of Marianna. They went first to the old wooden bridge over Waddell's Mill Creek. Levi and Sylvester drank some water from the spring-fed creek and the three then took turns using Levi's pistol to shoot at a tin can they had placed on one of the bridge rails. They had not eaten dinner, Dan Smith later testified, but had been drinking all afternoon.

After spending some time shooting at the tin can, they climbed back into the buggy, crossed the Chipola River at Bellamy Bridge and rode a few miles to Buckhorn Church. For whatever reason they decided to stop there and drink some more, so they spent about an hour outside the church drinking corn liquor. Now fully intoxicated, they decided to go "bathing" at Bellamy Bridge.

When the trio reached the bridge, however, they found that William Hall Milton was already there in his car with two ladies and some children. Instead of stopping and bothering this party, Smith and the two Harts crossed on over Bellamy Bridge and parked their buggy on what they called the "dam," an obvious reference to the earthen causeway that approached the bridge from the west. There they tied the mule to a tree and lifted the buggy out of the way so people would be able to pass, then walked down the seasonal creek to the point where it flowed into the Chipola River.

They looked at the water and Levi suggested that it was a good place to go "bathing," but Sylvester expressed concern over the number of logs in the river. The three decided to go back up to Bellamy Bridge and wait until Mr. Milton and his party left. While they were on their way back they saw Milton's car drive away. Unhitching the mule, they drove their buggy back across the bridge and parked on the east side before going down to swim in the river. According to Smith's later testimony, Levi Hart suggested to him that they drown Sylvester Hart while he was swimming in the river. Smith claimed that he refused and the three then got out of the river.

It did not take long however, for Sylvester to come down with what he thought was a "congestive chill." A fire was built on the bank of the river and he huddled near it to get warm. It was at this point, according to Smith, that "Levi Hart killed him with a pistol."

Dr. W.T. Burkett, who examined Sylvester Hart's body for the coroner's jury, later reported that the unfortunate man had been shot twice in the head. One bullet entered "a little above and back of the right ear," while the other entry wound was at the base of the skull on the back of the head. In short, Sylvester Hart had been executed. He fell forward and his left hand and arm were burned in the fire the three men had built on the riverbank.

Levi Hart and Dan Smith were both charged with the murder of Sylvester Hart. Smith was additionally charged with "counseling, aiding, hiring and procuring Levi Hart to do the killing." At a trial in Marianna, Smith testified against Hart and the latter man was convicted of murder and sent to the state prison at Raiford.

Some believe, however, that Sylvester's spirit still lingers at Bellamy Bridge and is responsible for some of the strange incidents there that are normally credited to the ghost of Elizabeth Jane Bellamy. Photographs taken of the murder site, for example, sometimes show a strange mist or anomaly at the spot where Sylvester Hart was murdered. Others believe that the strange lights seen at Bellamy Bridge at night are actually the ghost of the murdered moonshiner.

Whether such claims are true or not cannot be determined, but it is a fact that Sylvester Hart was the fourth person who suffered from a tragic death in some way associated with Bellamy Bridge. Perhaps the ghosts of all four are still there, roaming the night together in search of some peace they can never find.

Photographs

Ghost Images from Bellamy Bridge

Photographs: Ghost Images from Bellamy Bridge

Ball of Light streaks past Bellamy Bridge

An "Orb" is visible at Bellamy Bridge.

Mysterious Blue Light at Bellamy Bridge

Unexplained Image from near Bellamy Bridge

Photographs: Ghost Images from Bellamy Bridge

Unexplained Photograph from Bellamy Bridge Heritage Trail

An "Orb" from along Bellamy Bridge Heritage Trail

"Orb" at Bellamy Bridge reflects off the Chipola River

Mysterious Light at Bellamy Bridge illuminates the Ground

Photographs: Ghost Images from Bellamy Bridge

Strange Mist appears over Chipola River (Lower Right)

Enlarged View of Mist over Chipola River

Chapter Five

The History of Bellamy Bridge

The crossing point on the Chipola River that would later become the site of Bellamy Bridge has been in use for hundreds if not thousands of years. Fluted points and other stone artifacts left behind by prehistoric hunters indicate that humans entered the upper Chipola River valley thousands of years before the birth of Christ.

Called Paleoindians by archaeologists, these early people came to the area in pursuit of large animals such as the mastodon, a huge now-extinct mammal that looked much like a modern elephant. Scientists believe that the Florida of their time was much warmer and drier than it is today. The Chipola River and its tributary springs and streams would have been vital sources of water for both animals and humans. The Hays Spring Group just north of Bellamy Bridge and Waddells Mill Creek just to the south, for example, flowed during prehistoric times and artifacts from the Paleoindian time have been discovered along both.

The Hays Spring Group, in fact, revealed a nearly complete mastodon skeleton during the 1970s, some of the bones from which showed cut marks indicating that the animal had been butchered by Paleoindians. Unique fluted points dating from the Paleo era have been found in the Chipola River at Bellamy Bridge itself.

The mastodons and other large animals disappeared into extinction thousands of years ago, forcing the early people of the Chipola River to adapt their lifestyles. They focused on hunting such animals as deer, opossums, rabbits and the American bison (buffalo). The latter animal still lived in Jackson County as late as the 1600s. A herd was seen by Spanish explorers near today's Bellamy Bridge in 1686.

By around the time of Christ, the prehistoric Native Americans on the upper Chipola had developed the ability to make pottery and were engaged in agriculture and horticulture. They planted corn, squash, beans and other crops that we would recognize today, while also maintaining orchards of fruit and nut trees. Their houses were made with roofs thatched with palmetto fronds and walls built using the wattle and daub technique of weaving a framework that was then covered with clay to form a solid wall. Many of the trees and plants they used in building their homes, such as the palmetto, can still be seen at Bellamy Bridge today.

Artifacts from the vicinity of the bridge indicate that people lived there during what have been labeled the Weedon (Weeden) Island and Fort Walton time periods. The former era lasted from A.D. 400 to around A.D. 900 and was a period of advanced civilization among the Native Americans. They organized themselves into warrior chiefdoms and participated in organized religious practices and rituals. The latter era lasted from A.D. 900 to A.D. 1540 and in western Jackson County appears to have been marked by the arrival of an invading group, the Chacato.

Warlike and highly organized, the Chacato came down the Chipola River into what is now Jackson County sometime after around 1250 A.D. They established a fortified town and ceremonial center at the Waddell's Mill Pond site a few miles west of Bellamy Bridge. The discovery of Fort Walton Incised pottery eroding from the fill of the old causeway leading to the west end of Bellamy Bridge indicates that there was at least a small presence of Chacato people in the bridge vicinity. The pottery sherds were tempered with limestone in the same style as those found by archaeologists at Waddell's.

For some reason the Chacato lost faith in their religion and abandoned their ceremonial site at Waddell's Mill Pond shortly before the arrival of the Spanish in Florida during the 1500s. By the time Franciscan missionaries arrived in Jackson County in 1674, the Chacato were living in villages and small settlements stretching from what is now Houston County, Alabama, down into Washington County, Florida. The Chipola River formed something of a natural barrier for them and most of their settlements were located west of its course.

The early Spanish missionaries established Mission San Carlos and Mission San Nicolas among the Chacato in 1674 and also sometimes visited a third location they called San Antonio which, based on their descriptions of its location, must have been somewhere just northwest of present-day Campbellton. A powerful chief living in San Antonio, however, incited a rebellion against the

Spanish after the priests told him that to be a good Christian he would have to give up one of his two wives. He refused and violently drove them from Chacato territory.

The Spanish reprisal was swift and harsh. Troops and allied Apalachee Indians marched into the region and destroyed towns, burned fields and drove out Indian families not willing to convert to Christianity and live in close association with Franciscan friars. By the 1680s, most of western Jackson County was empty of people and the old village and mission sites began to return to nature.

This was the situation in 1686 when the first mention of the site where Bellamy Bridge stands today appeared in the records of Florida's early Spanish officials. Government officials in Cuba and Florida had heard rumors of a French settlement somewhere near the mouth of the Rio de Espiritu Santo ("River of the Holy Spirit"). We know this river today as the Mississippi. To verify these reports and order away any French intruders, the governor of Florida ordered a retired official named Marcos Delgado to lead an expedition west into the wilderness.

Little is known of Delgado other than that he had been a minor official in Florida's government and possibly was a cleric. At the time he was selected to lead the expedition, he ran a cattle ranch in the Apalachee Province near present-day Tallahassee. He organized his force at Mission San Luis, now beautifully restored in Tallahassee, and prepared to advance into the virtually unknown territory of western Florida and southern Alabama in the late summer of 1686. His total command consisted of 13 Spanish soldiers, one "Chata" interpreter and 40 Apalachee Indian warriors, 20 armed with firearms and 20 armed with bows and arrows.[1]

Delgado marched west from Mission San Luis in late August 1686 and by the first of September was at Mission San Carlos, a Spanish mission located in the vicinity of today's West Bank Overlook at the west end of the Jim Woodruff Dam near Sneads. Leaving San Carlos on September 2, 1686, he and his men followed the old trail northwest to today's Blue Springs, which he called "Calistoble" and described in glowing terms:

...Departing from the village of the chacatos (i.e. San Carlos) to the northwest on the road to Calistoble there is encountered at 5 leagues a spring of clear water which forms a river that has 48 feet of width. At the spring it is 36 feet in depth and the river below is from one yard to one yard and one-half in depth and is bordered by thickets of large cane about six inches thick.[2]

After stopping briefly to rest at Blue Springs, the expedition turned again to the northwest. Instead of following the old trail west across the Natural Bridge of the Chipola River at today's Florida Caverns State Park, Delgado moved up across the site of today's Marianna Municipal Airport and around Baltzell Spring, which he described as "a clayey place which has a small spring rising from a round rocky hole." Delgado's report indicates that a severe drought was affecting the region and many of the springs were barely flowing.[3]

Passing around the head of Baltzell Spring, the Spanish soldiers and their Apalachee allies worked their way back to the northwest and soon reached the Chipola River at or near the Bellamy Bridge site:

...[T]here is a clayey swamp and in its center a stream which has 36 feet of width and a depth of 6 feet and the swamp itself has half a league of breadth. It is thick and it was necessary to cut the path.[4]

Delgado's description of the Chipola River at Bellamy Bridge still stands today. The swamp there is about one-half of a league (roughly 1.5 miles) wide and at low water the river is of about the width and depth described in the Spanish report. The reasons for placing the crossing at or near Bellamy Bridge are simple. Had Delgado crossed to the south, he would have encountered a much wider swamp, multiple channels of the river and additional creeks not mentioned in his account. Had he crossed to the north, he also would have encountered a much wider swamp as well as the Hays Spring Group and Hays Spring Run, neither of which was mentioned in his account. From a geographic standpoint, only Bellamy Bridge and its immediate vicinity match his description. From a historical standpoint, the earliest surveys of Jackson County show an old trail leading northwest from Blue Springs. It passed around the head of Baltzell Spring and reached the Chipola River at the present Bellamy Bridge site. Since this trail predated the arrival of the first American settlers in the area, it probably was the one followed by Delgado.

After crossing the Chipola River at Bellamy Bridge and cutting his way through the floodplain swamp on the west side of the river to reach higher ground, Delgado marched on for about six miles to a place he described as "a plain of open pine woods that on its western side is bordered by a small spring." The spring at the head of Waddell's Mill Pond is almost exactly six miles from Bellamy Bridge and prior to the construction of the mill and dam during the early 1800s would have matched the description given by the Spanish leader.[5]

From there he marched on to what he described as a "miry place" (probably the head of Spring Branch near Jacob City) where he and his men "began to encounter buffaloes which are a kind of animal resembling cows." The account of American bison or buffaloes roaming northwestern Jackson County is difficult to imagine today, but early Spanish explorers of the area made mention of them several times.[6]

The explorers continued on to the site of the former Chacato village of San Antonio and from there made their way north into Alabama, eventually penetrating as far as the Upper Creek towns near present-day Montgomery. They failed, however, to reach the Mississippi River as the distance proved far more formidable than they had ever imagined. Delgado and his men eventually returned to San Luis, following their route back down through Alabama and across Jackson County.

Following the Delgado expedition, the Bellamy Bridge site fell into obscurity for more than 100 years. No mention of its immediate vicinity can be found during this period. Florida passed from Spain to Great Britain in 1763 following the end of the French and Indian War. English traders drifted into the Panhandle over the two decades that followed, as did Creek Indians who moved down from Alabama and Georgia. In 1778, during the American Revolution, a British military force crossed from Pensacola to St. Augustine, passing through northern Jackson County. The route of the expedition roughly followed today's State Highway 2, but a mapmaker named Joseph Purcell who accompanied the march produced a chart of the countryside that shows the present-day site of Bellamy Bridge. It is the oldest known representation of the upper Chipola River.[7]

One of the largest Creek towns established in Jackson County during the British era (1763-1783) was Ekanachatte or "Red Ground." Located on the west side of the Chattahoochee River at the site of today's Neal's Landing Park, Ekanachatte was a large and powerful town and its chiefs were known for their large herds of cattle and wealth.

Instead of keeping their cattle herds in close proximity to their town where the free roaming animals could damage their fields and orchards, the people of Ekanachatte established a cattle range to the west along the upper Chipola River. This range was along the west side of the river from the Forks of the Creek area where Cowarts and Marshall Creeks meet to form the Chipola down to where Waddell's Mill Creek flows into the river. The Bellamy Bridge site was included in this cattle range.

By 1817, the chief of Ekanachatte was a man called Econchattimico or "Red Ground King." Extremely wealthy and personally courageous, he reacted with outrage when U.S. troops attacked the Creek village of Fowltown in what is now Decatur County, Georgia. Econchattimico and his warriors sided with the alliance of Red Stick Creeks and Seminoles that went to war with the United States following the Fowltown incidents. Some of his warriors were believed to have been involved in the bloody attack on a U.S. Army boat commanded by Lieutenant Richard W. Scott of the 7th Infantry. That boat was ambushed at present-day Chattahoochee and of the 51 people on board, 34 men, 6 women and 4 children were killed. Another woman was captured and 4 men were badly wounded but escaped.

This retaliatory strike outraged U.S. officials, who blamed the Indians for starting the war. Major General Andrew Jackson was ordered to the Georgia border and given authorization to invade Spanish Florida to attack the warring Creeks and Seminoles. Ekanachatte became a target.

As part of the Army's effort to assemble forces for the planned invasion, thousands of Creek warriors were enrolled into the U.S. service. These were the so-called "McIntosh Creeks" who had sided with the United States against the Red Stick Creeks in the recent Creek War of 1813-1814. Led by Colonel William McIntosh, a mixed-race chief from Coweta (near Columbus, Georgia), they were hardened fighters with scores to settle against the Red Sticks who had fled down into Florida after their defeat at the Battle of Horseshoe Bend, Alabama.

Ordered to use his forces to sweep both sides of the Chattahoochee River and clear it of any enemy forces, McIntosh developed a plan to attack Ekanachatte as he advanced. Dividing his command in half, he sent roughly 900 men under the chief Captain Isaacs to scour the countryside east of the Chattahoochee, while he advanced with another 1,100 men down the west side of the river into Florida. His campaign was launched in early March 1818 and he encountered little opposition as he drove south.

On the morning of March 13, 1818, in what has been remembered as the Battle of Red Ground, McIntosh's warriors attacked the main town site at Neal's Landing. The inhabitants of Ekanachatte were cornered along the banks of the Chattahoochee River and more than 180 women and children as well as 53 warriors were taken prisoner. The violence began when the captured warriors tried to escape. In the gunfire that followed, 10 of Econchattimico's men were killed. The village was burned to the ground and its inhabitants carried away as prisoners of war.

The chief himself, however, was not among the prisoners. He and a small party of his warriors were on the Chipola when their village was attacked, tending to their cattle herds. Discovering their absence, McIntosh made immediate plans to capture them and their livestock and began a westward movement of his force. Probably following the old Pensacola – St. Augustine Road, he passed the site of present-day Malone and reached the east side of the Forks of the Creek swamp where Cowarts and Marshall Creek join to form the Chipola River. The water, however, was extremely high and the swamp was flooded:

I went down the creek Chaubellee the 12th day of March, about ten miles above the camp of Chunchattee Micco or Red Ground Chief, and the creek swamp was so bad we could not pass it for the high waters; my men had to leave their clothes and provisions, and swim better than one half of the swamp, about six miles wide; we marched within about two miles of his station, and the next morning we surrounded his place, but he was gone and we could not follow him till we could get some provisions we had left behind us.[8]

The "creek Chaubellee" mentioned by the Indian leader was the Chipola River, which was often spelled "Chaubellee" or "Chaubullee" in early accounts. McIntosh's report that he crossed what was undoubtedly the Forks of the Creek swamp and that the total distance he marched on the Chipola was ten miles is interesting. From the point where the old Pensacola – St. Augustine road reaches the east side of the swamp and begins its crossing, it is a little over five miles across the floodplain. From there down the west bank of the river to Bellamy Bridge is a little over four miles, with no natural obstacles in the way, making the total distance roughly ten miles.

This indicates that the "camp" or "station" of Econchattimico, as McIntosh termed it, was somewhere in the vicinity of Bellamy Bridge. Dr. Nancy White of the University of South Florida, who has conducted considerable archaeological research along the Chipola River, indicates that so far no Creek sites have been found along the upper river. Extensive study of the area around Bellamy Bridge, however, has not been done but is scheduled to take place in the near future as part of an archaeological survey of the upper Chipola River funded by the Northwest Florida Water Management District, which owns and manages much of the land on the west side of the river including the Bellamy Bridge Heritage Trail.

While Econchattimico's camp was abandoned when McIntosh attacked it, he sent a detachment of his command to follow the chief and his warriors. Led by Major Samuel Hawkins, the half-Creek son of the late U.S. Indian Agent

Benjamin Hawkins, this force attacked Econchattimico and about 30 of his warriors at an unspecified location somewhere beyond their camp. The chief, however, escaped, as did most of his remaining men, and remained carefully hidden until the end of the war. He then reassembled his people and established a new town site on the west side of the Chattahoochee River about 10 miles north of present-day Sneads. They lived there until 1838 when they were removed on the Trail of Tears to what is now Oklahoma.[9]

Almost as soon as the First Seminole War ended, American settlers began to drift down from Alabama into the edge of Spanish Florida. In 1819 a number of these families settled along Spring Creek, forming the basis of the modern town of Campbellton. Others settled on the old Ekanachatte fields at Neal's Landing. Because they needed a direct route for communicating with the U.S. Army post at Fort Scott on the lower Flint River, they opened a road from their settlement to the Chipola River. This pathway, which would later be called the Fort Road, intersected the river at today's Bellamy Bridge site. From there it originally followed the same path used more than 130 years earlier by Marcos Delgado, angling southeast to Blue Springs and from there east to the Apalachicola River between present-day Chattahoochee and Sneads.

By 1824, when the town of Greenwood was founded, a second pathway had been opened to connect the future Bellamy Bridge site with that town and eventually the Chattahoochee River at Port Jackson. This eventually became today's Fort and Bellamy Bridge Roads, although much of the road did not follow its current route until many years later.

Use of the crossing on a daily basis increased dramatically in 1821-1825 as lands in the vicinity were cleared for agricultural purposes. The rich lands along the Chipola River were ideal for growing sugarcane and in those early days it was expected that Florida would soon rival Cuba in the production of sugar. The land surrounding the future Bellamy Bridge site was cleared for the production of sugar in around 1820. Slaves did the backbreaking work of opening the floodplain swamp for farming, working through the heat of summer and floods of spring to accomplish the task. The swamps were infested with snakes and mosquitoes and the trees it was necessary to clear away were old growth cypress, gum and oak. Stumps still visible in the Bellamy Bridge vicinity indicate that some of these trees were more than ten feet thick.

The labor was done, however, and the fields were gradually opened. It was an invention developed just a few years earlier near Savannah, Georgia, that forever

46

changed the agricultural history of the land that surrounds Bellamy Bridge. In cooperation with Catharine Littlefield Greene, the widow of Revolutionary War hero Major General Nathanael Greene, a young inventor named Eli Whitney developed the mechanical cotton gin in 1793. The invention made the production of cotton on a large scale possible and highly profitable in the South and, some believe, assured the continuation and expansion of slavery in the Southern states. There is reason to believe that Mrs. Greene contributed significantly to the successful design of the cotton gin, but Whitney never gave credit for her role in its development.

Within three decades, "King Cotton" became the dominant cash crop of the South. As fields were expanded and then overused until yields began to decrease in Virginia and the Carolinas, plantation owners started to look into the Deep South for new lands and new opportunities. Florida had become a U.S. territory in 1821 and the northern part of the former Spanish colony was soon found to be ideal for the production of Sea Island cotton. With its rich lands and large tracts of available acreage, Jackson County attracted both wealthy planters and small farmers from all through the Carolinas and Georgia. Samuel and Edward Bellamy, as was noted in the early chapters, were among those who looked to rich Chipola River lands for the expansion of their family's fortune.

Dr. Edward C. Bellamy purchased a large tract of land surrounding Bellamy Bridge and relocated there in 1836. He and his wife, the former Ann Croom, built a beautiful home on a rise overlooking their vast estate and focused the efforts of their overseer and slaves on growing Sea Island cotton. Subsistence crops such as corn, rice and vegetables were also grown on the Bellamy plantation, which was actually a self-sustaining community. In addition to the main house, a smaller house was built for the overseer's family and a community of cabins was erected for the enslaved African American laborers who worked the farm. Other structures built during the early years of the plantation included corncribs, smokehouses, barns, stables, workshops, a blacksmith shop and a cotton gin and press.

Bellamy moved his large bales of cotton from the plantation down to the Natural Bridge of the Chipola River either by ox cart or small barge. A small port facility had been developed at the Natural Bridge and from there the cotton moved on down the river by barge or pole boat to the cotton warehouses at either Apalachicola or St. Joseph (today's Port St. Joe).

The Chipola River itself presented a natural barrier to these early farming efforts, as it was necessary for people, livestock and equipment to get back and forth across the stream. The old crossing at today's Bellamy Bridge site was used as a ford for a number of years, as at most seasons of the year it was shallow enough to be crossed on horseback. As the population of the county grew, however, the need for a bridge became readily apparent. While it has been thought that Bellamy Bridge was built in 1844, the year 1851 appears more likely.

Edward's brother, Samuel, was then battling for his financial life against his creditors. Heavily in debt following the collapse of the Union Bank of Florida, he tried to shelter his holdings from those engaged in or planning lawsuits against him by turning it over to Edward. A contract was executed between the two men on November 19, 1844:

...[T]he said Samuel C. Bellamy, in consideration of the premises as well as the sum of one dollar received, hath granted, bargained, sold, aliened, conveyed and confirmed, and by these presents doth herein grant, bargain, sell, convey, assign, transfer and deliver unto the said Edward Bellamy, all the property and estate hereafter described and specified, to wit: the following slaves, viz: Tony, Sally, Flora, Esop, and Cinda; also his stock of horses, mules, cattle and hogs, of which he is now in possession, and which cannot be more particularly described, together with his household and kitchen furniture, and all his personal effects of every name, nature and description, corn, wagons, carts, &c., also his crop of cotton of the present year, whether now in bales, in the gin house or in the field; also his right and interest in and to the contract for construction the bridge across the Chipola river near Marianna. To have and to hold all and singular, the property above described, and every particle thereof, to the said Edward Bellamy, his heirs and assigns forever.[10]

The indenture made between Samuel and Edward and quoted here was the first known document to mention a bridge over the Chipola River connected to the Bellamy name. While it has been generally thought that the bridge being built in the winter of 1844-1845 was the original Bellamy Bridge, it is unclear where the structure referred to in the indenture was actually located. It could have been the first bridge at today's Bellamy Bridge site or it could have been one of the two bridges built at Marianna during the same era. Samuel Bellamy actually lived in Marianna by 1844, while Edward still maintained residence on his plantation north of the city, so it would be logical for him to have been involved in a construction project benefiting the county seat. The 1844 bridge, then, most likely was one of the Marianna bridges and not the first Bellamy Bridge.

On February 2, 1850, however, the Board of County Commissioners for Jackson County approved a report by a group of road commissioners appointed to "view and lay out a road from near the plantation formerly owned by William B.

Wynns, crossing the Chipola near Doct. E.C. Bellamy, thence to Port Jackson on the Chattahoochee River." This road followed roughly the route of today's Highway 162, Bellamy Bridge, Fort and Green Roads from western Jackson County to Port Jackson, a long-faded riverboat landing on the Chattahoochee River. The county commissioners voted "that the same be declared a public road and that the road commissioners in the respective district through which the road runs be notified to take charge of same."[11]

The need for a bridge where this new road crossed the Chipola River was evident and on January 7, 1851, the commission appointed William F. Snelling, Richard Barnes and William R. Pettaway to "advertise, let out and examine timber for the building of a bridge across the Chipola River where the new road crosses said stream running from the Wynn Plantation to Port Jackson in line with Doct. E.C. Bellamy's avenue." Dr. Bellamy's avenue was the beautiful oak-tree lined passage known today as Bellamy Bridge Road. His stunning Terre Bonne plantation home stood along this avenue a few hundred yards east of the Chipola River.[12]

This authorization by the Board of County Commissioners was the first official document referring to Bellamy Bridge. The original appointment of Snelling, Barnes and Pettaway to examine timber was followed on May 27, 1851, by the appointment of Felix H.G. Long, Elijah Bryan and William Long to serve as commissioners to "let out a bridge across the Chipola River near Edward C. Bellamy's." These men were among the most prominent citizens of Jackson County at the time and their involvement in the project assured that it would be successfully completed.[13]

The successful bid for the project was submitted by Dr. Horace Ely and Bird B. Hathaway. A contract was awarded them on June 24, 1851, for the "building of a bridge across the Chipola River near Doct. E.C. Bellamy's Terre Bonne plantation." Ely and Hathaway, supervised by the Longs and Elijah Bryan, were the named builders of the first Bellamy Bridge. The actual labor, however, was probably performed by slaves.[14]

The builders agreed to make any necessary repairs to the bridge for four years after its completion, a clear expression of belief on their part that their work would stand the test of time. From the time the wooden span was finished, it became known as "Bellamy's Bridge" and later simply as "Bellamy Bridge." The structure was probably similar in construction to the one built by Dr. Ely across Dry Creek south of Marianna a few years later. His contract for that structure specified that it be 10-feet wide and built so that the road surface would be two feet above the high water mark. Support posts were to be planted into the ground which would support sleepers measuring 12 by 14 inches. The top of the bridge was planked and 3 by 4 inch hand rails were placed on each side. The original specifications for Bellamy Bridge have not been found.[15]

The original wooden Bellamy Bridge was completed in December 1851. Having inspected the structure, the county commissioners found that the work was well done and on December 16th they "ordered that the County Treasurer...pay to Doct. Horace Ely on his order the sum of Three hundred and forty-four dollars the same being for building the bridge across the Chipola River near Doct. E.C. Bellamy's Terre Bonne plantation."[16]

Dr. Bellamy still lived at Terre Bonne plantation when the bridge was completed, but over the next decade he lost his long fought legal battle with the estate of his brother, Samuel, and was forced to sell his home and property and relocate to a son's home in Mississippi. The Bellamy plantation at Bellamy Bridge came to an end not because of the Civil War, but before it ever started.

Bellamy Bridge, however, survived. It was the wooden bridge built by Ely and Bird that spanned the river at the important road crossing during the War Between the States. Confederate authorities knew by 1863 that the Sanders Gang and other Unionist guerrilla bands were operating from the Forks of the Creek swamp. This swamp is only 2-3 miles north of Bellamy Bridge and to protect the span from damage or destruction by the raiders, Confederate troops were occasionally stationed there. Among the units known to have been posted at the bridge during times of danger were Companies E and G, 5th Florida Cavalry; Captain Robert Chisolm's "Woodville Scouts" from the Alabama State Militia, and Captain Alexander Godwin's Campbellton Cavalry.

The most significant threat to the bridge developed on September 26-27, 1864, when a large force of Union cavalry and mounted infantry entered Jackson County from the west. Headed by Brigadier General Alexander Asboth, this column pushed back resistance from Godwin's small cavalry unit and occupied Campbellton on the afternoon of September 26th. As the Federals moved south the next morning, Confederate forces did not know at first whether they would continue down the Campbellton Road to Marianna or turn east on the road to Bellamy Bridge and Greenwood. Confederate cavalry commanded by Colonel Alexander Montgomery pulled back ahead of Asboth's force as it moved south and Captain Henry Robinson's Greenwood Club Cavalry was called out. Montgomery apparently was prepared to defend either Bellamy Bridge or Marianna as circumstances should dictate. Asboth advanced directly on Marianna, however, and Bellamy Bridge was spared. Montgomery's Confederates were defeated at the Battle of Marianna on the afternoon of September 27, 1864, and the city was heavily looted.

Open wooden bridges like the one built at the Bellamy plantation by Horace Ely and Bird Hathaway did not last long. Constantly exposed to rain, heat and cold, they rapidly deteriorated and had to be replaced about every twenty years. This proved to be about the lifespan of the 1851 bridge.

High water damaged the structure in the years after the Civil War and in 1869 the Board of County Commissioners, then appointed by Florida's Reconstruction era governor, approved the replacement of Bellamy Bridge. According to the commission minute books, Thomas Holliday was authorized to replace Bellamy Bridge on August 6, 1869. His contract also included the construction of a second "bridge across the long slough beyond Bellamy's Bridge."[17]

The addition of a second bridge to the contract marked the first known attempt by county officials to deal with the flooding that blocked access to the bridge from the west every spring and summer. The fields on the west bank of the Chipola had originally been cleared for the production of sugarcane and rice and were directly in the floodplain of the river. Whenever heavy rain brought the Chipola out of its banks, these fields and the road to the bridge that passed through them were covered with water. Traffic could not reach or leave the west end of the bridge until water levels had subsided enough for the road to dry out.

The access road to Bellamy Bridge was susceptible to flooding because a wet-weather stream flowed through a wide swamp there, crossing and re-crossing the roadway three times. The commissioners hoped to resolve this problem except in the worst of times by building a long wooden access bridge that would allow traffic to continue to move on the road to the bridge.

It would take three long years for Holliday and his workers to finish these bridges. The reason for this was partly because of the severity of the task of building a bridge through the swamp, but was likely more due to the horrible violence that shook Jackson County in the years 1869-1872. This was the era of the county's Reconstruction War, when local citizens battled the corrupt Northern officials who controlled Jackson County until they were driven out.

Despite his best efforts, Thomas Holliday was not able to report that he had completed the new bridges until November 1872. According to Vouchers #143 and #182, he was paid $594 for building Bellamy Bridge and the new access bridge and another $25 for flooring.[18]

It is worth noting that this new Bellamy Bridge was completed and paid for during the same winter (1872-1873) that the beautiful oak trees were planted at the Jackson County Courthouse in Marianna. It is a little known fact that the courthouse oaks were planted by a former slave named Easop or Aesop Bellamy for a total cost of $27. Well-known in Marianna, he had been among the slaves that Samuel C. Bellamy transferred to the custody of Dr. Edward C. Bellamy in 1844.

The second Bellamy Bridge, assuming the structure built by Samuel Bellamy in 1844 was at Marianna, did not last long. A heavy flood swept down the Chipola River in 1874. The main bridge at Marianna was badly damaged and both Bellamy Bridge and its "Slough Bridge" were destroyed.

Although details are scarce, the county commission minutes for April 8, 1874, indicate that E.S. Williams entered a bond on that date to rebuild the main Bellamy Bridge and the associated Slough Bridge. No details of his contract have been found and it is not known when he completed the project.[19]

This third wooden Bellamy Bridge was either of stronger construction than the 1872 structure or water levels did not again reach 1874 levels for several decades, as it continued to stand into the 20th century. By the time it started to seriously deteriorate, Jackson County's voters had approved a $300,000 bond sale to finance road improvements.

The bond referendum took place on August 1, 1911, and was intended primarily to fund the construction of hard surface or paved highways in the county. A portion of the money, however, was used to build the now famous and still-standing steel-frame Bellamy Bridge.[20]

According to the terms of an order issued by the Board of County Commissioners on September 21, 1911, the bonds were to be delivered for sale to investors in $25,000 increments, with $100,000 authorized to be sold between October 1, 1913, and January 1, 1914. The commissioners approving the sale were W.J. Singletary, Frank Peacock, J.F. Gammon and G.F. Williams. A fifth commissioner, G.E. Cartlidge, was absent on the day the order was approved.[21]

On January 17, 1914, the commissioners opened bids for the construction of "about ten miles of road" from Peri Landing to Nubbin Ridge Cemetery, about six miles of road from Greenwood to Bellamy Bridge and another six miles of road from Bellamy Bridge to Springfield on the Campbellton and Marianna Road. The winning bid of $275 per mile was submitted by W.F. "Flake" Chambliss on behalf of the firm of Chambliss & Whatley. A private citizen at the time, Chambliss later served as Sheriff of Jackson County. He and his partner agreed to finish the project by June 1, 1914.[22]

Peri Landing was located on the Chattahoochee River just north of present-day Parramore Landing Park. It was then an important steamboat landing where cargoes of cotton, turpentine rosin, lumber and other commodities were loaded aboard paddlewheel riverboats for transport either down to Apalachicola or up to Fort Gaines or Columbus, Georgia. The authorization of a major roadway leading from the landing to Nubbin Ridge Cemetery just east of Greenwood indicates the importance that the boomtown of Parramore had achieved in the county's politics. Although this section of the road can no longer be traveled in its entirety, it included sections of today's Parramore, Lovedale and Nubbin Ridge roads.

From the cemetery it connected with existing roadways for the short distance into Greenwood. The second six mile section then followed the route of today's Highway 162 and Bellamy Bridge Road to the Chipola River. From the west end of the bridge, the third section of the new road followed today's Bellamy Bridge Heritage Trail northwest for one-half mile to its intersection with what is now Highway 162, which it followed on to the Campbellton-Marianna Road.

Portions of this route, of course, already existed in the form of early roads and trails. As it approached the east end of Bellamy Bridge, for example, it passed down the beautiful canopy road described in 1850 as "Dr. Bellamy's Avenue." Other older roads were incorporated into the new wider road as well, but a large amount of new construction was also required. Commissioners Gammon and Peacock were appointed to lay off the new road in such a way that its route and construction would not interfere with the farms that lined it.[23]

Significant progress on the road was reported by February 21, 1914, when W.F. Chambliss was paid $1,173.90 for work completed to that date. In fact, work on roads throughout the county was progressing so well by February that the commissioners authorized the sale of another $100,000 in road bonds on February 9, 1914.[24]

The dirt road from the Chattahoochee River to Bellamy Bridge and then on to Springfield was completed on schedule by summer and on July 13, 1914, the county commission added a crown jewel to the project:

By Motion duly seconded it was ordered that an advertisement be placed in the Times Courier for a steel bridge to be constructed across Chipola River and Bellamy's Bridge. Specifications filed in Clk.'s office.[25]

The bids for the new bridge were opened on August 10, 1914. Converse Bridge & Steel Company submitted the low bid of $2,636, while Austin Brothers submitted the other and slightly higher bid of $2,774. Both amounts, however, were higher than the commissioners had expected and both bids were accordingly rejected. The two companies were then allowed to re-bid on the same day using the specifications originally issued for Peacock Bridge south of Marianna instead of those first proposed for the Bellamy project.[26]

After reviewing these changes, the companies submitted new bids with Converse proposing to complete the project for $2,389 and Austin Brothers offering to do the job for $2,560. The goal of the commissioners seems to have been to complete the project for under $2,500. The bid from Converse Bridge & Steel Company was accepted.[27]

The specifications of the contract called for the bridge to have a center length of 119 feet and a "clear width" of 12 feet. It was to be completed and ready for travel by November 1, 1914, a remarkably short period of time by today's standards. The commissioners themselves further accelerated the project by allocating $1,194 to cover the delivery of the material for building the bridge to the "nearest Railroad Station." W.H. Converse signed the contract on behalf of the company and W.J. Singletary, commission chairman, signed on behalf of the county.[28]

The new Bellamy Bridge was built in the Pratt through truss design, a method of construction that used a complicated system of steel beams, posts, plates and rods. The flooring itself was of heavy pine timbers and the entire structure was supported by four piers made by filling metal cylinders with concrete. These piers continue to support the steel-frame structure to this day, nearly one century after it was originally built.

The bridge still stands today, even though it was closed to vehicular traffic when Highway 162 and its concrete bridge were completed a short distance upstream in 1963. The wooden flooring deteriorated over the years and finally fell through into the Chipola River, where the timbers can still be seen on the bottom when the water is particularly low and clear. The steel-frame structure is still largely intact, however, making Bellamy Bridge the second oldest bridge of its type and one of the ten oldest bridges in Florida.

Instead of replacing the old "Slough Bridge" with a new span, the commissioners instead authorized the building of a long earthen causeway that stretched for roughly one-third of a mile from higher ground to the west end of the bridge. The construction of this causeway was done by Chambliss & Whatley using mule-drawn equipment and hand shovels. Some parts of it had been built during the construction projects of 1872 and 1874 and these sections were incorporated into the new causeway which was built by excavating dirt from along each side of the road corridor and piling it up along the center line of the road to create an elevated and useable surface. In places the causeway is only high enough to be barely discernible from the surrounding floodplain, but as it approaches the west end of the bridge it rises significantly higher.

To prevent the natural wet-weather stream from "blowing out" the causeway during times of high water, it was left open at two key points so the water could flow through the earthen wall or "dam" of the roadbed. Traffic moved across these gaps on wooden bridges that the county labeled Bellamy Bridges #2 and #3. A fourth wooden span, labeled Bellamy Bridge #4, crossed the wet-weather stream just west of the causeway. The heavy post and timber ruins of all three of these approach structures can still be seen today, although none of these bridges survives intact. In later years, pipe culverts were installed in the causeway at several other points to allow additional water flow during flood conditions.

Like the main bridge itself, this causeway was abandoned and closed when the new Highway 162 bridge was completed. Over the years it was reclaimed by the forest, although its earthen structure remains in remarkably good condition to this day.

It was the steel-frame bridge completed in 1914, of course, that became most closely associated with 20th and 21st century retellings of the ghost story. It stands today as an important landmark for generations of current and former Jackson County residents who love the history and folklore associated with the beautiful old structure.

---

[1] Gov. Don Juan Marquez Cabrera to Marcos Delgado, June 28, 1686, and Teniente Antonio Matheos to Gov. Cabrera, August 21, 1686, quoted in Mark F. Boyd, "The Expedition of Marcos Delgado from Apalache to the Upper Creek Country in 1686," *Florida Historical Quarterly*, Volume XVI, Number 1, July 1937, pp. 9-11.

[2] Marcos Delgado, Report, enclosed in Don Juan Marquez Cabrera to the King of Spain, January 5, 1686, *Florida Historical Quarterly*, Volume XVI, Number 1, July 1937, pp. 21-28.

[3] *Ibid.*

[4] *Ibid.*

[5] *Ibid.*

[6] *Ibid.*

[7] Registration Form for First American Road in Florida, National Register of Historic Places, National Park Service, Washington, D.C., Received August 17, 1988.

[8] William McIntosh to Major Daniel Hughes, dated "Chaubellee Creek" on March 16, 1818, printed in the *Camden Gazette*, April 11, 1818, p. 3.

[9] *Ibid.*; For a detailed account of Econchattimico's life in Jackson County after the First Seminole War, please see Dale Cox, *The History of Jackson County, Florida: The Early Years*, 2008.

[10] Indenture made between Samuel C. Bellamy and Edward C. Bellamy, November 19, 1844, in Mario D. Papy, Reporter, *Cases Argued and Adjudged in the Supreme Court of Florida at Terms Held in 1855*, Volume VI, No. 1, pp. 65-66.

[11] Jackson County Commission Minutes, February 5, 1850.

[12] Jackson County Commission Minutes, January 7, 1851.

[13] Jackson County Commission Minutes, May 27, 1851.

[14] Bond for Construction of Bridge executed by Bird B. Hathaway, Horace Ely & Others, January 10, 1852.

[15] *Ibid.*

[16] Jackson County Commission Minutes, December 16, 1851.

[17] Jackson County Commission Minutes, November 29, 1872.

[18] Voucher #143 and Voucher #182, Jackson County Commission Minutes, November 29, 1872.

[19] Jackson County Commission Minutes, April 8, 1874.

[20] Jackson County Commission Minutes Book G, 1913-1918, pp. 24-25.

[21] *Ibid.*

[22] Jackson County Commission Minutes Book G, 1913-1918, pp. 51-53.

[23] *Ibid.*

[24] *Ibid.*, p. 66.

[25] *Ibid.*, p. 112.

[26] *Ibid.*, pp. 121-122.

[27] *Ibid.*

[28] *Ibid.*

Photographs
Bellamy Bridge and Associated Sites

Support Post from One of the Original Wooden Bridges

Bellamy Bridge at High Water

Bellamy Bridge in ca. 1961

West End of Bellamy Bridge

Steel-Frame Structure of Bellamy Bridge

Bellamy Bridge, 2012

Bellamy Bridge, the 1914 Structure

Causeway Leading to Bellamy Bridge from the West

Ruins of Bellamy Bridge #2, One of the Original Approach Bridges

The Samuel Bellamy Mansion in Marianna was the largest private home in Florida when it was completed. It was here that legend says Samuel and Elizabeth were married and that a tragic wedding night accident took place.

Chapter Six

Bellamy Bridge Heritage Trail

Although it was no longer used for transportation purposes after 1963, Bellamy Bridge remained a much loved landmark in Jackson County. While the stories of its use as a party spot and "lover's lane" by the teenagers of the 1950s, 60s, 70s and 80s have achieved almost legendary status today, the bridge also created a wide array of less "notorious" memories for families from across the region.

Many residents remember that the bridge was a popular spot for fishing, camping, picnics and fish fries. Many people have fond memories of spending time with their fathers and mothers on the banks of the Chipola River at Bellamy Bridge. The steel-frame structure, now usually called the "old iron bridge," evokes childhood memories of family and home. Others have canoed, kayaked or boated down the river and beneath the bridge over the years, watching as it slowly deteriorated.

In an attempt to turn the historic site into a recreation spot, the Jackson County Commission secured federal grant funds during the mid-1970s and built a small park at Bellamy Bridge. While the county still held the road right-of-way on the east side of the bridge, the adjacent land was in the hands of a private owner. A lease agreement was negotiated and the park was opened adjoining and just north of the historic structure. A boat ramp was installed, as were picnic tables and other amenities.

Lack of money for maintenance and security, however, doomed the project and the park quickly deteriorated due to neglect and vandalism. It became a nighttime hangout spot for teenagers and the landowner, Jimmy McArthur of Malone, became concerned over drug use and other illicit activities taking place at the bridge as well as his liability should someone be hurt on the property. The park was eventually closed and the lease ended. The site where the park existed is now on the private lands of the McArthur Trust and is closed to the public.

Despite a failed effort during the late 1980s to maintain public access to the bridge itself via the county's road right-of-way, Jackson County abandoned several hundred yards of the road leading to Bellamy Bridge and the property reverted to the private landowners. Only the bridge itself remained a county property, but all public access to it from the east down Bellamy Bridge Road came to an end. The road was blocked and since has been fenced and allowed to return to nature.

For more than thirty years Bellamy Bridge stood isolated but not forgotten. The ghost story continued to attract attention and trespassers often slipped across the fences to see the bridge, but just as often were warned away by landowners or law enforcement officers.

The land encompassing the floodplain swamp on the west side of the bridge, came into public ownership even as public access was being lost to the east end of the structure. The Northwest Florida Water Management District has been engaged in a decades-long effort to acquire, preserve and restore land along the Chipola River as well as its springs and tributaries. This noteworthy project led to the acquisition by the District of thousands of acres on the west side of the Chipola River. Included in the purchase was the old road bed and causeway leading to Bellamy Bridge.

When the Northwest Florida Water Management District first acquired the property on the west side of the bridge, much of the flood plain had been clear cut of the pine timber that had grown there after the old fields were abandoned. Putting in place a visionary plan to restore the swamp to its original purpose and natural function, Bill Cleckley and other employees of the District undertook a laborious effort to replant the lands with original species of trees and plants. Today, with those trees and plants reaching maturity, the formerly clear cut fields have taken on an unparalleled beauty and ecological significance.

Now managed as part of the Upper Chipola Management Area, the former fields of the Terre Bonne Plantation have been returned to their natural beauty. Unless otherwise posted, all District lands are open to the public daily for purposes ranging from fishing and hunting (when in season) to hiking, bird watching and enjoying nature.

The acquisition of the lands west of the river by the District created a unique opportunity to preserve Bellamy Bridge and its access road as important historic sites. By 2012, the Jackson County Parks Department was interested in somehow saving Bellamy Bridge and reopening to the public. A pro bono engineering study was prepared by UNAKA Consulting of Tallahassee to determine the condition of the bridge. Among the ideas under consideration was the actual relocation of the historic structure from its original site to a new greenway park area near Marianna where it would be used as a foot bridge to allow hikers to cross the Chipola River.

The idea of relocating the bridge to a new location inspired the dreams of some and the disappointment of others. Among people with a long association for and love of the historic structure and its folklore, the idea of it being picked up by crane or helicopter and moved away was unacceptable. A swell of public support for saving the bridge at its original location and reopening public access to it began to grow during the spring and summer of 2012. This led to the forming of a loosely organized group that dubbed itself the "Friends of Bellamy Bridge." The objective of the assemblage of like-minded people was to develop a heritage trail leading across Northwest Florida Water Management District lands to the west end of Bellamy Bridge.

As the idea began to take shape, Chuck Hatcher, director of parks for Jackson County merged his previous efforts with the new initiative. A meeting was arranged with District staff to discuss the trail concept and an onsite visit to Bellamy Bridge took place. The afternoon walk generated massive enthusiasm for the idea and a plan was developed under which the Friends group would offer to help build, maintain and fund improvements for the trail, Jackson County would provide on-site supervision and the Water Management District would allow use of the lands and provide the overall review and approval process for the project.

Over a four-week period in the late summer of 2012, the author and Chuck Hatcher presented an overview of the proposed trail to the District's lands committee and to the Board of County Commissioners for Jackson County. With remarkable speed, both bodies voted unanimous approval for the project. The Board of Directors of the Northwest Florida Water Management District also gave unanimous approval and the Bellamy Bridge Heritage Trail became a reality.

Crews from the Jackson County Parks Department, volunteers from the Friends of Bellamy Bridge and inmates and staff from the Jackson County Correctional Facility spent a number of days in September and October of 2012 clearing brush and briars from the trail corridor, building a new parking lot on Highway 162, putting up safety rails, building a temporary footbridge and adding new decorative fencing around the parking area and trail entrance. By late October, all of the first phase of the three phase project had been completed.

With both a full moon and Halloween in the last week of October, plans were made to introduce the public to the new heritage trail with a series of guided night walks down the new pathway to the historic bridge. Guides were trained and the tours began with a visit from the Blue Springs Chapter, Children of the American Revolution, on the evening of October 21, 2012, and a special "VIP Tour" for supporters and public officials the following morning.

These two tours began ten days of activity on the trail that culminated with three nights of "Bellamy Bridge Ghost Walks" on October 27, 28 and 31. More than 1,000 people attended these preview events, some coming from as far away as Texas, Virginia and even Michigan to walk the new trail and learn about the history and folklore that surrounds the bridge, especially the tragic story of the best known "ghost of Bellamy Bridge," Elizabeth Jane Bellamy.

To the surprise of all involved, including the author, the Ghost of Bellamy Bridge made an unexpected appearance during the tours. On the nights of October 26 and 27, a mysterious blue light appeared in the steel-frame skeleton of the old bridge. Pale and hazy, it remained there for a few seconds and then faded away. To date, no one has been able to offer a reasonable explanation other than that perhaps Elizabeth was welcoming company after so many years of loneliness. Numerous photographs were taken of it, one of which can be seen in the Ghost Photographs section of this volume.

The Bellamy Bridge Heritage Trail officially opened to the public on November 1, 2012, nighty-eight years to the day after the original completion date of the steel-frame bridge. Accessed from a parking lot located on the south side of Highway 162, 1/10th of a mile west of the modern Chipola River bridge, the trail leads down the historic causeway and roadbed to Bellamy Bridge. The distance is just over 2,600 feet or almost exactly one-half mile. Benches have been installed along the way to provide spots to rest and enjoy the stunning beauty of the restored floodplain forest and swamp.

The ruins of Bellamy Bridges #2 and #3 can be seen along the trail, as can some of the original live oak trees from Dr. Edward C. Bellamy's avenue. At the bridge itself, an overlook has been created and branches have been trimmed back to create a beautiful vista of Bellamy Bridge. Immediately to the left of the bridge on the water's edge can be seen a stunning old-growth cypress tree that is several hundred years old. The tree was growing when Marcos Delgado and his men crossed the Chipola River more than 300 years ago.

Future plans for the trail include the completion of two foot-bridges over the gaps in the historic causeway where bridges #2 and #3 once stood. These spans will be constructed in such a way as to preserve the ruins of the original approach bridges. The process of placing interpretive signs along the trail is already underway. Boy Scouts have installed small tree identification markers to help nature lovers identify some of the more noteworthy trees. A major informational kiosk for the trail entrance has been funded by the Jackson County Tourist Development Council and will provide information on the trail, Bellamy Bridge and the crossing of the Chipola River by Marcos Delgado. Two additional interpretive panels have been funded for the overlook at the bridge itself and will tell the story of Delgado's crossing, of Bellamy Bridge and of the ghost story. Design work on these interpretive points was underway as this book went to press.

The Bellamy Bridge Heritage Trail is open to the public during daylight hours. Public access is not allowed after dark, but special guided tours can be arranged at no cost by contacting either the Jackson County Parks Department or the Jackson County Tourism Office.

Section Two

Ghosts & Monsters of Jackson County, Florida

Chapter Seven
The Graceville Spook Lights

Along a section of railroad track on the west side of Graceville, a pair of lights are said to appear on certain nights and under the right conditions. Always seen from a distance, they first appear in very dim form, but then brighten considerably before fading away into the darkness. The only real story attached to them is that long ago two people, a man and a woman, died on the railroad trestle over Holmes Creek and that the lights are their ghosts.

Such "ghost lights" or "spook lights" have been reported in locations across the South. In North Carolina, for example, people see the Maco Light, while Georgia has the well-known Surrency Spooklight. Arkansas is home to the Gurdon and Dover Lights and in Missouri people report seeing the well-documented Seneca Light. There are many others.

The Graceville Spook Lights are unique from many of these sightings in that they always appear as a pair. The obvious question surrounding them, aside from their true nature, is: Did a man and woman ever die on the trestle over Holmes Creek? The answer is yes.

In 1910, Graceville was a booming community that was making a name for itself in newspapers across the nation. The railroad had arrived there just eight years before, opening a whole new market for the farms of northwestern Jackson County. Incorporated with the arrival of the railroad, the city quickly became the largest watermelon shipping point in the world. In addition to its important train station, by 1910 Graceville also had churches, a school, a cotton gin, warehouses, stores, a newspaper, a town hall and a jail.

The trouble started in August of that year when a man named Edward Christian was accused of stealing a watch from one of the town's physicians. The doctor swore out a warrant for Christian's arrest and went with Deputy Sheriff Allen Burns to identify the suspect so Burns could take him into custody. Christian was found at the home of a woman named Hattie Bowman:

...When Burns, accompanied by the physician, went to Christian's home to make the arrest he was greeted by a volley of shots, one bullet striking Burns in the breast and another in the arm. His condition is considered critical.[1]

The shooting of Deputy Burns sparked outrage in the Graceville community. Burns was white and both Christian and Bowman were black. The racial element of the shooting was not lost on the local people. Adding fuel to the fire was the fact that the town was still new and raw and those were the days of high profile lynchings in America. A man named Doc Peters had been lynched in Cottondale earlier in the summer and newspapers were filled with lurid accounts of mob-orchestrated lynchings from all over the country.

Although they are often portrayed today as a Southern phenomenon or "Southern Justice," lynchings were in no way confined to the South. Lynch mobs carried out their mode of "justice" in far-flung places across the nation, from New England to the South and from the Midwest to the West.

Frightened over the consequences he faced for his alleged role in the shooting of Deputy Burns, Edward Christian fled Graceville and went to Dothan. Hattie Bowman, who had been in the house at the time that Christian opened fire, was quickly taken into custody by local authorities and lodged in the Graceville City Jail. Posses were organized to search for Christian, but he was located instead by officers in Dothan who took him into custody. On September 1, 1910, he was returned to Graceville and lodged in the city jail, where Hattie Bowman was already being held. The news of his arrival electrified the town and it was not long before a plan developed to deal with the pair without the time and expense of a courtroom trial.

That night, with no advance warning, a large mob surged into the street outside the jail. The guards were overpowered, although there was little they could do in the face of the crowd that confronted them, and men forced their way into the facility. Christian and Bowman were dragged from their cells and nooses placed around their necks.

The crowd then moved down to the railroad tracks, leading the two terrified prisoners by the nooses around their necks. Bowman and Christian were marched out onto the trestle that had been built so the trains could cross Holmes Creek into Graceville. The loose ends of the ropes were tied to the beams of the trestle and the two unfortunate prisoners were kicked off the bridge and into eternity:

Graceville, Fla., Sept. 3. – Dangling from a trestle just outside the town, this morning, were found the bodies of Ed. Christian, a negro, charged with shooting Deputy Sheriff Allen Burns, and Hattie Bowman, a negress, who had been arrested on the charge of being implicated in the crime.[2]

The bodies of Christian and Bowman were cut down and buried, but those involved in the lynching were never identified. Although the double lynching received coverage in newspapers as far-flung as *The New York Times* and the *Toledo Blade*, it drew the greatest attention in Alabama. The L&N Railroad that ended in Graceville connected to the main rail network in Alabama instead of Florida and news of the incident spread up the line to the newspapers of that state. The *Montgomery Advertiser*, in fact, led the call for a thorough investigation of the hangings. On September 7th, the editors of the *Advertiser* called for the Florida Railroad Commission to look into the matter, as the deaths had taken place on the railroad right of way.

As such incidents usually do, though, the deaths of Edward Christian and Hattie Bowman gradually faded away from the public consciousness. While there would be more lynchings in Jackson County, no others took place in Graceville.

It seems reasonable to believe that, while the details of the lynching have for the most part been forgotten, the deaths of Christian and Bowman are remembered in the story of the Graceville Spook Lights. But are these lights supernatural or is there a reasonable explanation for them?

There have been scientific investigations of similar lights in other locations, most notably the famed Seneca or Hornet Spooklight in the far southwestern corner of Missouri. While these investigations were not conclusive, students from the University of Arkansas were able to duplicate the Missouri spooklight by moving a car along a distant road at twilight and after dark. The rolling nature of the hills in the vicinity allowed the car lights to be seen from a great distance through gaps or low spots in the intervening ridges.

Could a similar situation be creating the Graceville Spook Lights? It is certainly possible. The lights are most often seen from near the intersection of

Jones Road and State Road 2 just west of Graceville. A review of the U.S. Geological Survey topographic map shows that a view directly up the railroad tracks from this point encounters not the ridge on the opposite side of Holmes Creek, but a gap in that ridge created by the course of Little Creek. Behind this gap pass several city streets and even State Road 77. Lights from cars on the roads could be flashing across the valley of Holmes Creek and to the high point on the opposite side from which the ghost lights are usually seen.

Is this the explanation for the Graceville Spook Lights? It would take a detailed study to find out. For now, the mystery of the lights continues and it is certainly possible that it never will be solved.

---

[1] *The New York Times*, September 3, 1910.
[2] *Toledo Blade*, September 8, 1910.

Chapter Eight

The Two Egg Stump Jumper

Unusual stories are part of the charm of the historic community of Two Egg, located in the heart of Jackson County about fourteen miles northeast of Marianna. The one they tell of a strange, hair-covered creature often spotted in an area just seven miles northeast of the main crossroads may just take the cake.

Multiple witnesses now claim to have seen something that can only be described as a monster roaming the woods and swamps between downtown Two Egg and the Chattahoochee River. While the accounts vary somewhat, the strange creature can best be described as a "mini" Bigfoot.

Two accounts reported on the website www.twoeggfla.com originated from within one mile of each other, although both were independent and there was no connection between the witnesses.

The first eyewitness described hearing a noise outside his home late at night. Going outside to investigate, he says he was stunned to see "something upright, running away on two legs." The creature or monster was of about normal human height and was pale in color. According to the witness, it ran into a marshy area and could be heard splashing away through a pond.

An investigation of the area the next morning revealed tracks leading straight down through the mud into the pond, but it was impossible to determine what might have left them. They were not human footprints, but were too large for a deer or other similar animal. The soft, wet mud had obscured too much of their appearance to determine anything more about their source.

The second sighting took place about three-fourths of a mile southwest of the first one and near the intersection of Circle Hill and Oak Grove Roads. An eyewitness saw a small upright creature with long hair running away through a marshy area. It was smaller than average human height, but was running on two legs. The individual relating the story to the website described it as a "mini" Bigfoot. The sightings have prompted a great deal of speculation in the area, where strange howlings are often heard in the night.

It is worth noting that tales of small Bigfoot-like creatures are not exactly new in Florida. Residents of South and Central Florida have been reporting an animal they call the "skunk ape" for years. They are, however, very new to the Two Egg area. The speculation over what it could be increased on April 2, 2010, when a wildlife camera placed in the swamps near Parramore Landing (nine miles east of the Two Egg crossroads) captured the indistinct image of a creature standing upright. Was it a bear? Or did the Stump Jumper make an unexpected appearance?

The residents of the area tell the stories with a bit of tongue in cheek, but witnesses plainly believe they saw something out of the ordinary. "I got a really strange feeling that I was seeing something that wasn't supposed to be there," said one. Others described a similar sensation. Meanwhile, hunters in the area of the sightings have described encountering an unbelievably foul smell for which they could determine no source.

The sightings faded as summer turned into fall and fall into winter, but by late spring of 2011, the Stump Jumper was back. The latest known sighting as this book was being prepared for press took place on Oak Grove Road in the Parramore community during the first week of June of that year. A driver was traveling north on the road from its intersection with Circle Hill Road when she saw a strange creature run across the dirt road through the glow of her headlights.

Although her glimpse of the monster was brief, the eyewitness said that it appeared to have long shaggy hair, was gray in color and close to or slightly below the height of a grown man, although much more bulky. This is consistent with other sightings of the creature, which is usually described as a grayish or brownish "mini-Bigfoot" like monster, but with a round head instead of the "peaked" head often described by eyewitnesses who say they have seen Bigfoot. At least one eyewitness, however, also reported that the Stump Jumper has a "raccoon-like tail." The latest eyewitness did not observe a noticeable tail, but admitted she was so stunned by its sudden appearance that she might not have noticed one.

The sighting was typical of others that have taken place in the area. The creature has almost always been seen in and near the small, swampy ponds north of Parramore crossroads and usually only as it is crossing the road or running away into the darkness. It has never been seen in daylight hours, prompting those who believe in it to assume it is nocturnal in its habits.

What made the 2011 sighting different, however, was that it left behind some physical evidence. A search of the area on the day after the sighting revealed unusual footprints running across a plowed fire lane about 200 yards from the location where the sighting took place. They were about 8 inches long , but were not shaped like either human footprints or the unusual prints often attributed to Bigfoot. The feet that left behind these prints appeared to have a large "big toes" or thumbs and then two smaller toes. The result was an almost "hand-like" print, minus two fingers or toes.

Talk of the Two Egg Stump Jumper continues in the Parramore area, but so far as is known there have been no sightings since the one in June 2011.

Chapter Nine

The Headless Indian Chiefs of Sneads

Although few people remember it today, there is an old legend about a spot on the Apalachicola River near Sneads that is said to be haunted by the restless spirits of two Indian chiefs. It is said that on foggy nights, their headless bodies can be seen standing by the river, evidently hoping for the return of their heads.

Whether you believe in their supernatural aspects or not, old stories like this one are important reminders of the days before radio and television when long winter evenings were spent telling stories by firelight. As such they represent an important part of Southern culture and often have a basis in some real incident. The story of the headless Indian chiefs, for example, preserves the dim memory of real events that took place along the Apalachicola River during 1830s. The area bordering the river just north of today's Gulf Power Plant was then a Native American village called "Walker's Town."

The village was part of a reservation set aside by the Treaty of Moultrie Creek for a chief called the "Mulatto King" by the U.S. Government and the "Black King" by the Spanish. He had lived in this spot for many years and gained his name because his father had been a black Spanish trader. He died at his home during the early 1830s.

Following the death of the Mulatto King, the leadership of the village passed to his nephew, a man named John Walker. He stayed on good terms with the neighboring whites and was well known to many Floridians in his day.

During the early years of the Second Seminole War (1835-1842), a large party of refugee Creeks came down into Florida from Alabama. After engaging in a series of battles with white troops, they agreed to surrender if they would be allowed to keep their arms and live with other Native Americans until a boat could be arranged to transport them to the new Indian Territory in what is now Oklahoma. John Walker offered to let them live at his village and they assembled there in 1837.

One of their leaders was a well-regarded chief named Coa-Hadjo. Shortly after he arrived at Walker's Town, however, Coa-Hadjo became embroiled in an argument with one of Walker's followers, a warrior named Lewis. The argument grew out of control and Lewis drew a knife and stabbed Coa-Hadjo. When their chief died from his wounds, Coa-Hadjo's followers then dragged Lewis from his home and executed him by firing squad according to traditional Creek law.

It would seem that the story might end there. The people of Walker's Town left for Oklahoma less than one year later and most of Coa-Hadjo's former followers, now led by the chief Pascofa, fled back into the swamps to continue their war against the whites.

Strangely, though, the heads of both Coa-Hadjo and Lewis soon wound up in the possession of Dr. Joseph R. Buchanan of Cincinnati, Ohio. He wrote a letter from Pensacola in 1839 indicating that he had acquired the skulls of the two men, along with the skull of the long-dead chief Mulatto King as well. Apparently he either dug them up himself or purchased them from some local citizen who did so.

Dr. Buchanan believed he could learn the personality and other aspects of the dead by studying their skulls. He wrote a brief report on the "information" he gathered from the skulls of Coa-Hadjo, Mulatto King and Lewis and then added them to his macabre collection.

The old Apalachicola River legend preserves the memory of this bizarre grave-robbing incident and the headless Indian chiefs of the story are undoubtedly Coa-Hadjo and Mulatto King. What eventually became of their heads is not known.

Chapter Ten

The Wild Man of Ocheesee Pond

Jackson County is blessed with an abundance of alleged sightings of the monster that some call Bigfoot or Sasquatch. In South Florida it is generally known as the Skunk Ape, while to the west in Walton County stories are told of the Swamp Booger.

Reports of these creatures have come from virtually all parts of the county. In the swamps and remote woods around Parramore and Two Egg in eastern Jackson County, for example, many stories are told of the Two Egg "Stump Jumper," a sort of mini-bigfoot that is often seen in the headlights of cars at night or lurking in the darkness around rural homes. Similar sightings have been reported in the swamps along the Chipola River, particularly in the Forks of the Creek area between Malone and Campbellton. Other reports have come from the swamps along the Apalachicola River and the vast cypress forests of Ocheesee Pond.

It was in this last locality in 1884 that a party of searchers pulled off one of the few documented captures of a Bigfoot-like creature that in the parlance of those days was called the "Wild Man of the Woods."

Sightings of the Wild Man were nothing new in South of the 19th century. Indians told early settlers of a strange man-like creature that roamed remote swamps and woods. Covered with hair and much taller than normal humans, the monster was considered dangerous and most who encountered him would not approach him.

As the frontiers spread westward and the population of the Southern states grew, so too did the numbers of reports of encounters with the Wild Man. In Arkansas, settlers told of a Wild Man that chased cattle and left footprints more than 17-inches long. Similar stories were told in North Georgia, where a Wild Man was spotted at Snodgrass Hill on the Chickamauga Battlefield and chased along the ridges of Lookout Mountain. Another supposedly even killed a man in Fannin County, Georgia, during the years after the Civil War.

These and other similar stories long predated the first accounts of the Sasquatch of the Pacific Northwest and from their volume and detail indicate that Bigfoot was a fixture of life in the South many years before people began finding giant footprints or taking grainy film in the mountains of Washington and Oregon. It was therefore not considered huge news when people began spotting a Wild Man in the thick cypress swamps of Ocheesee Pond in 1883.

Located below Grand Ridge and Sneads in the southeast corner of Jackson County, Ocheesee Pond was a focal point for early settlers. More than three miles long and nearly that distance wide, the clear water pond fills a vast shallow basin. While there are some sections of clear water, primarily along its southernmost reaches, most of Ocheesee Pond is covered with a dense growth of cypress and other swamp trees. It is a strikingly beautiful place, but the swamps can easily feel a bit foreboding as well.

The Wild Man traditionally favored such dense and swampy locations, but in 1883 local residents nevertheless were surprised when their neighbors began reporting encounters and sightings of one of the creatures. He seemed to live on berries and other edibles that grew wild in and around the pond and was often seen swimming or wading as he moved from island to island. He tried his best to stay away from humans, but his cries often shattered the nighttime stillness of the farms and homes nestled along the shores of the pond.

As the number of sightings increased, so too did concerns about the safety of local families. Residents of the pond area gathered and discussed the situation and finally decided that an effort should be launched to capture or drive off the monster. Men assembled with guns, boats and horses and a plan was devised by which they would converge on the creature's last reported location from various directions at once.

Many of these men had served only twenty years before in the Confederate Army and some among them had even taken part in the swamp fighting of the Second Seminole War. They knew the pond well and had seen far scarier things in their lifetimes than a man covered in hair. They also knew something of tactics and deployed their forces in such a way as would produce results. It did not take them long to find their prey and on August 18, 1884, startling news went out from Columbus, Georgia:

News brought by the steamer Amos Hays from Lower River is to the effect that the wild man captured in Ocheecee Swamp, near Chattahoochee, and carried to Tallahassee, did not belong to a Florida asylum, and that all inquiry proved unavailing to identify him. He had been swimming in Ocheecee Lake, from island to island, and when taken was entirely destitute of clothing, emaciated, and covered with a phenomenal growth of hair. He could give no account of himself, and the theory is that he escaped from an asylum of some other state, and spent his time in the woods, living on berries, &c.[1]

The *Amos Hays* was a paddlewheel steamboat the operated on the Apalachicola, Chattahoochee and Flint Rivers, carrying cargo and passengers to and from Apalachicola on the Gulf, Bainbridge on the Flint and Columbus on the Chattahoochee, as well as various points in between. Since she offered rapid communication to Columbus, it was that point that the story began to be wired out to other locations. It did not take it long before it began appearing in newspapers as far away as New York, Indiana and Michigan.[2]

Other reports followed, but the details were consistent. The captured Wild Man acted insane, was covered with a thick growth of hair and had lived deep in the swamps in a state of total wildness.

The newspapers of the time, however, were silent on the eventual fate of the Ocheesee Pond Wild Man. Despite the fact that his body was covered in thick hair, he was human enough in appearance that his captors believed that he probably had escaped from an asylum. They carried him first, undoubtedly strongly bound, to Chattahoochee. The old arsenal there recently had been converted into a state insane asylum and it was thought that perhaps the "Wild Man" had escaped from there. Guards and doctors at the facility were quick to turn them away, however, with news that he had never been inside their walls.

Chattahoochee was linked by rail with Tallahassee and the Wild Man was carried by train to the state capital where it was hoped that additional information might be obtained. No other state, however, reported the escape or absence of a mentally ill person matching his description. From that point, he seems to disappear from the written record.

What became of the Wild Man of Ocheesee Pond and what, exactly, was he? As of this writing, the answers to those questions remain in the realm of mystery. No trace of him can be found after he was taken to Tallahassee and his eventual fate is unknown. Most likely he was ordered back to the state mental health facility in Chattahoochee as a "John Doe." If so, he might well have lived out his life there and the old hospital cemetery could well contain a grave that holds the answer to the mystery over whether Bigfoot is a real creature or just an intriguing myth.

The best that can be said about what the "Wild Man" may have been is that he was covered with "a phenomenal growth of hair," appeared human and was clearly judged to be insane by his captors. This description, of course, matches perfectly with modern eyewitness accounts of Bigfoot. The creature is usually described to be covered with thick hair and often as extremely human in appearance, but with an air of "wildness."

Did the Wild Man of Ocheesee Pond eventually secure his freedom and return to the swamps from which he came? Or did he live out the rest of his days behind the walls of a facility for the insane? The answers may exist, but will require much more research to reveal.

---

[1] *The New York Times*, August 19, 1884.
[2] *Ibid.*

Chapter Eleven

The Ghost of St. Luke's Episcopal Church

A church might seem like an odd place to encounter a ghost, but in reality many historic sanctuaries are the focal points for stories of hauntings and mysterious events. Considering the horrors that took place at St. Luke's Episcopal Church during the Battle of Marianna, perhaps it is not surprising that stories of a ghost were common there well into the latter half of the 20th century.

According to accounts given by several elderly members of the church in the 1980s, St. Luke's was said to be haunted by the shadowy figure of a Confederate soldier. He supposedly frequented the lower levels of the church and could be seen there at night, drifting along and apparently oblivious to those who witnessed him. The figure was invariably described as an "old man, with a long beard." He carried a musket and never spoke or otherwise recognized that he was appearing to people in a time other than his own.[1]

It seems somehow appropriate that such a story surrounds the church. It was, after all, the centerpiece of one of the most tragic and desperate scenes in Florida history.[2]

On September 27, 1864, having spent nine days in the saddle on their way from Pensacola Bay, the Union soldiers of Brigadier General Alexander Asboth attacked Marianna. The various sources differ as to the exact time of the attack. Some say it was at 10 a.m., some say 11 a.m. and others even say 12 noon. This is

---

[2] For a detailed account of the Battle of Marianna, please see Dale Cox, *The Battle of Marianna, Florida*, Expanded Edition, 2011.

common in accounts of Civil War battles as men in those days set their watches by the time in their home towns. Our modern concept of time zones did not come into effect until later years.

What is known, however, is that the Union attack came from two directions at once. A flanking party of mounted men came around a logging path that followed the route of today's Kelson Avenue and entered town by way of Caledonia Street. The man body of the Federals, meanwhile, charged directly up what is now West Lafayette Street.

The Confederates, led by Colonel Alexander B. Montgomery, had anticipated the attack up West Lafayette, but not the flanking movement around the north side of town. When the colonel and his cavalrymen were forced back from the edge of town, they were driven up Lafayette and directly into the flanking party that had taken up positions around the courthouse. Fighting hand to hand for their lives there, they were unable to do anything to assist the men and boys of the local home guard, who were positioned behind the trees, fences, buildings and shrubs along the stretch of West Lafayette between St. Luke's and today's intersection with Russ Street (then called Ely Corner).

In a fierce encounter, the home guards were driven back from their initial positions along both sides of the street. The main body of the Marianna Home Guard, along with scattered men from other units, fell back into the strong board fence that then surrounded the St. Luke's Churchyard. A Federal bayonet charge drove them from the fence into the cemetery behind the church, where they held out far longer than expected, despite the fact that they were completely surrounded. The men and boys of Marianna continued to fight, often firing from behind the tombstones of their loved ones, until they ran low on ammunition and were forced to surrender.

As the home guards were forced back, a handful took shelter inside St. Luke's Church and the nearby homes of Mrs. Caroline Hunter and Dr. R.A. Sanders. Eyewitness accounts note that some of these men were firing down on the Union soldiers from the steeple of the church. When the rest of the home guards surrendered, they refused to give up their arms. A standoff then ensued, with the men and boys in the church shooting at the Federal soldiers swarming the street and grounds and the Union officers alternated between trying to talk them out and ordering their men to keep up their fire.

General Asboth had been severely wounded by this stage of the battle and leadership of the attacking forces had fallen to his second-in-command, Colonel Ladislas L. Zulavsky. A nephew of the famed Hungarian freedom fighter Lagos Kossuth, Zulavsky had fled to the United States after the collapse of the freedom movement in Hungary in 1848. An experienced officer, he served the Union during the war and by 1864 was the colonel of the 82nd U.S. Colored Troops, a detachment of which was at the Battle of Marianna.

A fiery officer (he had once threatened to impale one of his own officers with a sword), Zulavsky decided to burn the church in order to drive out the defenders still holed up inside. Armstrong Purdee, an 8-year-old child liberated from slavery at the Waddell Plantation, watched from the back of one of the Union soldier's horses as the fire was set:

All of the soldiers were off their horses. Orders were given to fire the church. Three men, two with long poles, and one with what seemed to me to be a can, threw something up on the church and the other two having something on the end of their poles, seemed to rub it as high as the poles would reach, after which something like twisted paper was lighted and placed to whatever was put on the church and it blazed up. Men were shot down as they came out of the building.[2]

When the fire was set, at least five men were still inside the church. Woody Nickels, Jack Myrick and Littleton Myrick were young friends who had gone into the battle together. Along with them was 22-year-old John C. Carter, who had been discharged from the 6th Florida Infantry after suffering a severe wound at the Battle of Chickamauga, and 76-year-old Francis Allen, a senior deacon and Sunday school leader from the Greenwood Baptist Church. Both men had turned out to fight when the alarm was sounded, Carter with the Marianna Home Guard and Allen with the Greenwood Club Cavalry.

The scene at the church quickly turned from bad to horrific. Battle eyewitness Mary Lawrence Beeman later described what happened as the defenders came out of the doors and windows of the burning church:

...Some were wounded and fell so near the flames that they were literally roasted. Woody and Littleton M., with his brother Jack, started out together. Littleton M. was shot through the head, dead. Woody's leg was broken: he fell, but he struggled to get from the heat. Unable to rise, he was dragging himself along by catching at the rank grass with his hand. He had reached a monument nearby, when he was set upon by a negro. Those wounded nigh unto death, and utterly defenceless, already scorched by the fearful heat, there prone at his enemy's feet he lay. O God! That some who loved him could have been near to ward off that brutal blow which sunk deep into his temple.[3]

As Beeman described, Woody Nickels was killed with a blow to the head from a musket book as he lay with his arms wrapped around the monument of Major Jesse Robinson, a soldier of the War of 1812, which still stands just in front of the church.

Two of the men, John C. Carter and Francis Allen, never even made it out of St. Luke's. According to Surgeon Henry Robinson of the Confederate forces, their bodies were found in the ashes of the church after the battle. Both men had been so consumed by the fire that they could only be identified by metal items they had carried on them. Lewis Atkins, who came up on the night after the battle with the Calhoun County Home Guard, later described how the stench of the burned human flesh was so bad that he almost could not stand it.

The church was, of course, rebuilt on the same site in the years after the war and was even rebuilt again after the replacement structure burned due to a lightning strike during the 1940s. The present edifice is beautiful and appropriate. It also looks much like the church burned during the Battle of Marianna and stands on the same site.

Of the two men found inside the ruins of the church, only Francis Allen would match the description of the elderly ghost. At age 76, he was one of the oldest men to fight in the battle. Since the ghost is described as an elderly man with a long beard, it seems likely that it represents Mr. Allen, although no photograph or portrait of him is known to survive.

The ghost of St. Luke's Episcopal Church, as described by those who seen it, does not seem to be a conscious entity, but instead is one of those manifestations that always seem to follow a set pattern. These types of ghosts are difficult to categorize, but are sometimes called residual hauntings. They do not seem to be conscious entities or spirits. Instead they are almost like dim movies that replay themselves over and over under the right conditions. Could they be photographs on air? It is an interesting possibility that might explain why they always follow the same pattern, seemingly oblivious to the fact that the world has changed around them.

Whatever the truth, the ghost of St. Luke's seems to have faded quite a bit over time. Of a number of current members of the church that I questioned about the ghost while writing this book, only one was aware of his existence. Perhaps as time goes on, he will fade away entirely, taking with him a poignant memory of human suffering at the Battle of Marianna, Florida.

[1] Eyewitness accounts provided by three members of St. Luke's Episcopal Church, July 1986.

[2] Armstrong Purdee, "Eyewitness Tells of Burning of Church," *The Kalender*, June 1, 1931.

[3] Mary Lawrence Beeman, "Killed in Cold Blood," *Our Women in the War: The Lives They Lived, The Deaths They Died*, published by the Charleston *News and Courier*, 1885.

Chapter Twelve
Ghosts of the Russ House

The historic Russ House in Marianna is one of the most beautiful old homes in Florida. And some claim it is one of the most haunted!

Located at 4318 West Lafayette Street (U.S. 90) in Marianna, the historic structure at the time of this writing was the home of the Jackson County Chamber of Commerce and served as the county's official visitor center. Its future as a public resource, however, was in doubt. Even so, it will likely remain one of the most photographed structures in Marianna.

In fact, thousands of photographs have been taken of the old house. Most simply capture its classic beauty, but others show something else entirely. Often what looks like a shadowy figure can be seen standing in the window of the tower on top of the house. This is particularly curious as the tower functions as a skylight and has no floor.

Various groups of ghost hunters, in fact, say that several ghosts haunt the Russ House. Among them is reported to be the ghost of its builder, Joseph W. Russ, Jr.

The historic home was built in 1895 by Russ, who was a successful Marianna merchant with large land holdings in the county. The house was originally Victorian in appearance. The beautiful columns and rounded two-story porches were added during a renovation in 1910, but for more than 100 years now they have graced the gentle hill that overlooks the intersection of Lafayette and Russ Streets in Marianna.

The yard of the house is hallowed ground. Although the Russ House itself had not been built at the time, the intersection of Lafayette and Russ Streets was where the heaviest fighting of the Battle of Marianna began on September 27, 1864. The area was then known as Ely Corner and it was here that the Union 2nd Maine Cavalry rode into heavy fire laid down by Confederate troops. Several men were killed or wounded within view of the house.

Over the years, the house's glory days faded and it became a weathered gray place with an undeniably gloomy feel to it. Its appearance alone sparked many stories of ghosts and the supernatural. While most of these stories were without foundation, some former residents say that strange things really did happen in the Russ House. Others were less certain.

The house has definitely seen its share of tragedy over the years. There were scandals over marriages, a fortune was lost in the great crash of 1929 and the home's builder, Joseph W. Russ, Jr., committed suicide in 1930. He was evidently despondent over the loss of the family fortune in the Great Depression. Attempts to negotiate a bank loan to keep the estate intact had failed. Whether or not he actually killed himself in the house is disputed. Some say that he did, but others say the incident took place at a different house on nearby Green Street. Either way, many believe that the dapper businessman still haunts the rooms and hallways of his beloved home.

Former residents have described mysterious sounds and unexplained sights in the house. One, in fact, recommended that Chamber of Commerce employees think twice about working alone in the house after dark. A photograph taken in what formerly was an upstairs bedroom revealed a mysterious shadow in front of a fireplace.

Paranormal groups have investigated the Russ House, but have drawn differing conclusions about whether it is haunted. One group left convinced that it was, reporting that there was evidence that at least two ghosts haunted the house. Another concluded that the house was not haunted, but that the presence of two people could be felt there.

Employees and visitors have described unusual scents, cold spots, strange noises and even the apparition of a man with a mustache at the top of the staircase. Joseph W. Russ, Jr., it should be noted, had a mustache. Others describe "creepy" feelings that came over them while working in the house alone and at least one said that she once heard footsteps across the floor of the room above where she was working.

The mystery of whether the house is really haunted remains unsolved.

The Ghost of St. Luke's Episcopal Church

Chapter Thirteen
Ghosts of Old Parramore

What would a ghost town be without a few real ghosts? If the stories that have been told there are to be believed, then the vanished riverboat town of Old Parramore in Jackson County has no shortage of former residents who haven't quite seen fit to move on from their old homes and community.

Founded during the years after the War Between the States by a mixture of Confederate veterans and former slaves, Parramore grew into a thriving community by the end of the 19th century. Paddlewheel steamboat traffic on the Chattahoochee River was in its heyday and the community's landings became important ports for both loading and unloading cargo from the beautiful "floating palaces." As the landings thrived, so too did the surrounding area and a commercial center grew around the intersection of today's Parramore and Oak Grove Roads on the high ground inland from the river itself.

At its height, Parramore was home to a half-dozen stores as well as a post office, cotton gin, sawmill, gristmill, blacksmith shop and several major naval stores operations. Black smoke could be seen pouring from the smokestacks of the turpentine stills that surrounded the town as raw sap from longleaf pines was cooked down into rosin. Untold hundreds and even thousands of barrels of rosin were shipped out from Parramore's landings for use in making paint and a variety of other products.

Parramore was also an important shipping point for cotton, lumber and even boxes filled catfish pulled straight from the Chattahoochee River. The market for catfish in the Midwest, particularly in Kansas City, was huge and diners there enjoyed Parramore fish in untold numbers.

By the 1920s, however, Old Parramore was in to decline. Competition from the railroads was slowing driving the riverboat companies out of business. The construction of modern highways and increased use of trucks as a means of moving cargo further accelerated the end of the paddlewheel steamboats and by 1941, when the Japanese bombing of Pearl Harbor brought the United States into World War II, the *John W. Callahan, Jr.* had ended its runs. It was the last of the real paddlewheel steamboats to run the river. The U.S. Army Corps of Engineers snagboat *Montgomery* would continue to be seen on the Chattahoochee through the 1970s, but it was a government vessel that carried no commercial cargo.[1]

What remained of Parramore by that time rapidly faded away. The turpentine stills were reclaimed by the forests and the houses where the workers that operated them once lived slowly deteriorated and collapsed in on themselves. Only a few scatterings of brick now mark the sites were lines of small cabins once stood as housing for the families of the men who did the backbreaking labor of collecting the sap from the trees or running the stills where it was cooked down even on the hottest days of the year.

The stores disappeared one by one. The steam engine from the sawmill was carried to Greenwood for use in a mill there. The warehouse at Peri Landing (pronounced "Pea-Rye"), one of the primary riverboat landings for the community, rotted away and the landing itself became overgrown and forgotten. Houses, barns and stables vanished and today only a few traces survive to remind the casual visitor that the town of Parramore ever existed. It is a true Florida ghost town.

Numerous ghost stories are told about the Parramore area, which also is noted as the stomping grounds of the famed "Two Egg Stump Jumper." Perhaps the oldest revolves around the home of William Henry Cox, which no longer stands but once faced Oak Grove Road on the northern edge of the settlement.

A big old dogtrot style house with a detached kitchen, the structure was the home of William Henry Cox who at the age of 15 had fought in the Battle of Marianna as a member of the Greenwood Club Cavalry. His unit was made up of school boys from the Union Academy in Greenwood and his captain was also his teacher, Henry J. Robinson. The boys helped roll back the first Union attack on Marianna, but were eventually driven up Lafayette Street by a second Federal charge. One of their lieutenants, Dr. M.A. Butler, was killed in the fighting along Market Street in Marianna. Cox and most of the boys, however, made it across the

Chipola River bridge on the east side of town and assisted other Confederates in tearing up the flooring of the span to prevent the Union troops from crossing after them. They then engaged in an afternoon long skirmish with blue-coated soldiers on the opposite bank of the river.[2]

A man with an appreciation for good humor, Cox later answered queries from family members about his role in the battle with the response the he had "fired one shot and run." His reference, of course, was to the standard 19th century cavalry tactic of advancing on the enemy and firing a volley, then falling back to allow the mounted soldiers a chance to reload their muzzle-loading firearms. When appalled relatives would ask why he had run, however, Cox would reply with a glimmer in his eye, "Them people in Marianna ain't never done nothing for me!"

During his lifetime, William Henry Cox found numerous interesting ways of supporting his family. He built large rafts of logs from old growth longleaf pines and floated them down the river to Apalachicola where they were sold to the shipyards. He then used a portion of the proceeds to catch a riverboat back home. He also farmed, but was best known in the community as a well digger.

He enjoyed being down at the bottom of wells so much, in fact, that he often climbed down into his own well to escape the noise and chaos created by his ten children. His oldest grandson, Thomas Cox, later recalled that he had often been told how children would be sent out to jiggle the water bucket rope to let their father know it was time to come up from the bottom of the well for supper.

A large celebration was held at Cox's house every Fourth of July, with music, food and dancing. The house was center for life in the northern edge of Parramore and even as an elderly man, its owner enjoyed spending time with his friends, family and neighbors. He also enjoyed, his grandchildren later recalled, taking long walks just after dark to enjoy the cool fresh air of the evening. In fact, several of them remembered that he liked his walks so much, that he kept on taking them – even after he was dead.

William Henry Cox died on July 15, 1913, but not long after he was laid to rest in his grave at nearby Circle Hill (Pine Level) Cemetery, his family noticed something strange. Each night at the exact time he had made his nightly walks, the old front gate in front of the house could be heard squeaking open and then slamming shut.

At first it was written off as the wind, but it continued to happen. As weeks turned into months and months turned into years, the family could draw only one conclusion: William Henry (or "Uncle Bill" as many called him) was continuing his nightly walks. The ghost walks continued, it is said, until the old house and its surrounding fence were torn down in 1939.

Or perhaps they continue to this day, only no one is able to hear the passage of the ghost from the yard because the old fence and its squeaky gate were removed? Dogs in the community can become skittish shortly after dark and often are be seen barking at the road that runs by the old house site, even when nothing (or no one) can be seen there.

One room of the old William Henry Cox house can still be seen today, its detached kitchen. A simple "board and batten" structure, it stands where it did when the 19th century dogtrot house was dismantled in 1939. It is one of the last standing original structures of Old Parramore.

Locally called the "Old Kitchen," it has a unique history. Built in around 1880 as local people reasserted control over their government in the years after Jackson County's violent Reconstruction War, the little wood building originally served as a one-room schoolhouse for the community. In fact, it is believed to be the oldest school building in Jackson County and one of the oldest still standing in Florida.

When built it was located about one-quarter of a mile west of where it stands today and was part of a small schoolyard that included the building itself, a rudimentary baseball field and an outhouse. Students attending the school studied from the Rose Primer and sat on simple plank benches. They were of all ages, from the youngest child to teenagers already hardened to life by farm labor, and they all studied in the single room of the schoolhouse. Heat was provided by a wood-burning stove. The windows had shutters instead of glass and, since there was no electricity, there was no electric light.

First known as the Cox School and later as the Watts School (after the nearby Watts Turpentine Still), the little schoolhouse remained in use for its original purpose until the early 20th century when it was consolidated with other area one-room schools to form the new multi-room Parramore School. That school was eventually replaced by Central School, the ruins of which can still be seen on Circle Hill Road in Parramore.

Its history as a one-room school over, the building was moved one-quarter mile northeast of its original site to serve as a detached kitchen for a house on what became known as "Jonah Hill." This name was derived from Jonah of the Bible, the man swallowed by a whale, because the hill was considered to be an unlucky place. One of the houses that stood there was blown away by a tornado that left debris and smoked meat as far away as Seminole County, Georgia, across the Chattahoochee River. Another house on the hill was destroyed by fire.

After serving as a kitchen on Jonah Hill for roughly one decade or so, the little schoolhouse was moved again, this time to the William Henry Cox home a few hundred yards south where the previous kitchen was in need of replacement. Thomas Cox was a small boy when the structure was moved, but later could remember how the men of the community joined together to roll the little building to its present location using pine poles as rollers. Mules were hooked to one end of the structure and the men used long poles as levers on the other end to slowly roll it forward down the road.

It remained in use as a detached kitchen until 1939 when the William Henry Cox house was dismantled and replaced with a new house built 50 or so feet to the north by his son, Charles Whitman Cox. In fact, family members recall that they all moved into the one-room kitchen for a few weeks while the new house was being built so that lumber and timbers from the old house could be used in the construction project.

Since 1939, the "Old Kitchen" has served as a barn and storage building. Some believe, however, that it continues to serve as a schoolhouse for a group of energetic children from long ago. Laughs and noises have been heard from in and around the building at night, neighborhood dogs have a preoccupation with trying to get inside of it and strange bumps and rattles sometimes are heard from the interior of the building.

Do the playful ghosts of children from more than one century ago haunt the little schoolhouse? Or is it a place where the imagination plays tricks on the ears of eyewitnesses in the dark of night? The answers are as enigmatic as the questions.

Just across the yard from the Old Kitchen and the site of the William Henry Cox house stands the 1939 home of Charles Whitman Cox. Built as a replacement house by Charles and Ola Cox, it remains in use today as a private residence. It also has something of a macabre history and some believe that it may be the most haunted house in Jackson County.

The residence was built in the final days of Old Parramore using longleaf pine timber cut from the farm and milled into lumber down the road at the Parramore sawmill, as well as beams and some wide planks from the older house. It was one of the first new houses built in the area after the darkest days of the Great Depression and as such it became a community gathering place for the continuation of an old Southern custom: "sitting up with the dead."

In the days before modern medical advances, the recently departed sometimes came "back from the dead." Although there were a few cases that still cannot be explained, this most often happened because people fell into deep comas and were thought to be dead when they really were not. Sometimes they came back to consciousness before they were buried, other times they did not. In fact, in St. Augustine it was a custom to attach one end of a string to the fingers of the newly dead and the other end to a small bell placed on their grave. The night watchmen then listened for any sounds of bells ringing in the cemetery so the dead could be saved if they came back to life.

The fear of being buried while still alive was very real for people of earlier generations and was the real reason for another Southern custom, sitting up with the dead. On the night after someone died, their friends and relatives would often gather in the living room or parlor of a house. The deceased person would be stretched out in an open coffin and their loved ones would literally spend the night watching over the body to make sure it showed no signs of life. As with the little bells in St. Augustine, it was a way of making sure that no one was buried before they were really dead.

Since it was the newest house in Parramore when it was completed in 1939, the old Charles W. Cox house became a common location for "sitting up with the dead." The bodies not just of family members but of neighbors as well were stretched out in the living room of the house and loved ones sat up through the night to watch over them. There were no recorded instances of anyone coming back from the dead there, but over the first two decades of its existence the house sheltered far more dead bodies than are ever seen in most homes. Perhaps this is part of the reason that the "Old House," as it is known in the community, is also said to have more than its share of ghosts.

The strange incidents there began after Ola Cox, one of the original owners, died in 1966. Within a matter of weeks after her death, relatives living nearby noticed one evening that the lights were on in the house. No one was known to have visited that day, but the house was carefully inspected and the lights were turned off. The next night, though, it happened again. And it continued to happen.

In fact, each time that the house has been vacant over the years, similar things have happened. Lights will inexplicably be found on, things will be moved around inside and sometimes it is even said that shadows can be seen moving across the windows. Such events are common in houses said to be haunted, but in the case of the "old house," there is much more to the story.

During the late 1980s, a family living in the house encountered a bizarre series of episodes. The incidents began when the mother and father would awaken in the night to the sounds of someone eating. Low voices could be heard as if a family was quietly talking around a table and the distinct sounds of eating utensils clicking against plates could be heard. Even stranger was the fact the sounds came not from what was then the dining room, but from an area that had been the dining room before the interior was remodeled in the mid-1980s. Upon inspection, nothing would be found and no further sounds would disturb the house for the night. The sounds, however, would return the next night.

Strange sounds in the night were just the beginning. As time passed and the family adapted to the mysterious late night diners, other unexplained things began to happen.

On a winter's night the house suddenly bolted awake to the sound of shrill screams coming from the bedroom of the family's two small boys. Both parents rushed into the room to find the oldest child, around 5 years old, standing at the head of his bed with his sheets gathered around him, screaming uncontrollably. The father tried to calm his son but it took almost an hour to do so. During this time the child spoke incoherently about "the woman" or "that woman."

When the boy finally calmed enough that his story could be understood, he told his parents that a woman with long gray hair and wearing a long white nightgown had come into his room and kept trying to reach out to him. At one point she even tried to calm his fears by dancing for him. She had been plainly visible to him in the dark of the bedroom, apparently glowing from a light within or illuminated by light from an unseen source.

The incident was bizarre, but even more bizarre was the fact that the woman seen by the young boy immediately reminded neighbors of Ola Cox, one of the original owners of the house. Born Ola Avery in Decatur County, Georgia, on June 18, 1891, she was a direct descendent of William Brown or Efau Emathla ("Dog Warrior"), chief of the Yuchi or Euchee branch of the Lower Creeks. She and Charles Cox had married in 1911 and by the time they built the house in 1939, they had 10 children ranging in ages from 26 to 5.[3]

There are two facts most commonly remembered by her children and grandchildren. The first is that she had a seemingly boundless love for children and always wanted to be around them, even in the last months of her life when she was extremely ill. The second is that before bed each night, she would walk through the house closing every window – regardless of the season or temperature – worried that if a rain shower blew up it might soak her linoleum, a floor covering of which she was especially proud. She always did this after putting on her long white cotton gown and brushing out her long gray hair.[4]

It also is remembered of her that she was so concerned about mosquitoes that after the windows and doors were all sealed tightly for the night, she would walk through every room spraying insect repellent from an old-fashioned sprayer that had to be pumped through its long handle. Family members who visited her as children have vivid memories of the clouds of insecticide left behind from this nightly ritual. The practice, of course, reflected her own childhood worries about mosquito-borne diseases such as malaria, the very sickness that once claimed the life of Elizabeth Jane Bellamy.[5]

Was the specter that disturbed the sleep of the young boy simply a bad dream? Or was it the ghost of Ola Cox reaching out to the child from beyond the grave? The answer depends largely on what you believe about such things.

The strange happenings in the old Cox house did not stop there. A few months later, the parents returned home from an event to find their teenage babysitter outside on the front steps in the dark, with both of the children playing on the front porch. Visibly shaken, she would not immediately explain what had happened other than to say that something had terrified her. She later detailed how, while sitting in the living room, she had looked up to see the dark figure of a man watching her. She grabbed the children and rushed outside and would not go back into the house until the parents had returned and even then did so only with great apprehension. The living room, it will be recalled, was where the people of the community used to gather to "sit up with the dead."

The disturbances at the house continued for years. Even after the family moved out, the lights would mysteriously turn themselves on at night. The structure has since been sold and extensively remodeled inside. Several different families have lived in it over the years, but none of the recent occupants report any unusual occurrences there.

The stories of ghosts in Old Parramore do not stop on the Cox farm. In fact there are numerous other tales:

- The ruins of old Central School are said to be haunted by the ghosts of students and teachers from long ago. It is claimed that classes continue there, even though the structure burned down in an accidental fire many decades ago. Curiously, photographs taken of the ruins have revealed strange anomalies that look almost like streaking balls of light.
- The old oak tree near the Peri Landing site where Claude Neal was lynched in 1934 is said to be haunted by the man's ghost. Strange moans and lights have been reported coming from the area of the tree during the night and local legend holds that nothing will grow on any spot where the man's blood was spilled.

- The first structure of Circle Hill Baptist Church, which no longer stands, was said to be haunted. Long-time residents of the community said during the 1980s that they remembered hearing stories of bumps, moans and clanking chains being heard from inside the old frame structure. It was dismantled when the current church was built more than 50 years ago.

- During the 1960s and 1970s, it was possible to stand on the grounds behind Circle Hill Baptist Church and see two distinct lights glowing in the woods about one-half mile to the north. The strange white lights originated from a low hilltop where two children who died from fever during the Depression era are buried. As the woods between the church grounds and the burial site grew during the 1980s and 1990s, the lights were obscured and no longer could be seen. The pines were harvested in the fall of 2012 and the lights are once again visible.

---

[1] For a detailed account of the life of Parramore, please see *Old Parramore: The History of a Florida Ghost Town*, by Dale Cox.

[2] For a detailed account of the fighting, please see *The Battle of Marianna, Florida (Expanded Edition)*, by Dale Cox.

[3] Pearl Cox, "Cox Family: Charles W. and Ola Avery," Book Three in a series of unpublished volumes on the Cox family lineage, n.d.

[4] Memories recited by Lizzie (Cox) George, Alfred Cox, Ruby (Cox) Anderson, Emma (Cox) White, Pearl Cox, Jimmy George, Sandra Donaldson and others, 1986 – present.

[5] *Ibid.*

Chapter Fourteen
Ghost of the Ely-Criglar Mansion

THE HISTORIC ELY-CRIGLAR MANSION IN MARIANNA is one of the most beautiful homes in the United States. Built in around 1840, when the Second Seminole War was still in its fury, the house has weathered battle, hurricanes, civil unrest and the commercial expansion of the city to survive as an elegant and charming reminder of other times. It is listed on the National Register of Historic Places and the Historic American Buildings Survey. It also is haunted by the mysterious ghost of a woman wearing a long dark skirt and a high-necked white blouse.

No one knows exactly who the woman could be, although it is generally agreed that she is the figure of a someone who must have had an association with the house during the antebellum era. She is said to be quite beautiful and always appears formally attired. She is described as a woman of obvious elegance and her appearances usually occur on or near the staircase that rises from the central hallway of the home.

Located at 242 West Lafayette Street in Marianna, the Ely-Criglar Mansion was built by Francis R. Ely, a prominent Marianna merchant and planter. When the house was finished in around 1840, it stood on what was then the western edge of Marianna. Located on a spacious estate, it was built with security in mind because small war parties of Creek Indians were then moving through the Florida Panhandle. Attacks on homes or isolated travelers were common as the Native

Americans battled for their survival in a forgotten part of the Second Seminole War (1835-1842).

Its location on the edge of town made the Ely home vulnerable to such attack so it was designed to function not just as a residence, but as a fort of sorts as well. The thick brick walls of the 48' by 50' central portion of the house extend from the rafters of the attic all the way down into the ground. The exterior walls are so thick that no small arms fire, such as that from the small caliber rifles carried by Creek warriors of that time, could penetrate through into the house. The house was further strengthened by the fact that its interior walls were also extremely thick and ran from attic down into the foundation. Even if a war party of Indians might breach one of the rooms, the defenders of the house could retreat into another room and still be just as secure.

The windows were originally equipped with shutters made of wood so thick that a rifle or musket bullet of the time could not be fired through them. When closed, along with the similarly built doors, they rendered the home perfectly secure from attack.

The walls and shutters came to the test on September 27, 1864, when Union troops headed by Brigadier General Alexander Asboth attacked the Confederate defenders of Marianna. Commanded by Colonel Alexander Montgomery, the Southern cavalry formed for battle across Ely Corner, today's intersection of Lafayette, Russ and St. Andrews Streets, where the Campbellton and St. Andrew Bay Roads met in 1864. Named for the Ely Estate, the corner was the scene of heavy fighting during the Battle of Marianna.[1]

The angle of the Union attack up the Campbellton Road was such that the front of the Ely-Criglar Mansion was struck by a shower of bullets. Possibly the most battle-scarred private home still standing in Florida, the brickwork of the house shows scores of indentations from where it was struck by rounds from the Burnside carbines carried by the Union soldiers of the 2nd Maine Cavalry. At least one artillery shell from a 12-pounder light howitzer was fired at the house during the battle. It struck in the attic and plowed a path through the rafters, but fortunately did not explode.[2]

Because the ghost sometimes appears in doorways or sheltered nooks within the house, there has been speculation that she was in the structure while the Battle of Marianna was raging outside. This idea is not as far-fetched as it might sound. All along Lafayette Street, civilians and often even children were left alone while their husbands, sons and fathers battled the Federal troops in the streets of the city.

Just up the street from the Ely-Criglar Mansion, in fact, 12-year-old Lizzie Lawrence and her little sister, Lee, were left alone in the home of Reverend

R.C.B. Lawrence while he took up his gun and went to fight the attacking Yankees as a member of Captain Jesse J. Norwood's Marianna Home Guard. Lizzie later wrote an account of their experiences in which she described how the two girls stayed hidden in the house during the battle, listening to the sounds of the gunfire coming from their own front yard.

At a neighboring house, two young girls slipped outside to watch the battle. To obtain a better view of the fighting in the street, they climbed to the roof of the family's chicken coop. They stayed there until the "buzzing of the bees" around them became so bad that they had to climb back down and return to the safety of their home. The "bees" that so bothered the girls that day actually were the bullets being fired by the soldiers fighting in the street and yards. The rounds from many Civil War weapons gave off distinct buzzing sounds as they flew towards their targets. It was extremely fortunate that neither of the young girls was injured.

So far as is known, none of the noncombatants on the battlefield was hurt. They did suffer the trauma of finding their loved ones shot down, bayoneted, beaten with musket butts or even burned to death in the ashes of St. Luke's Episcopal Church. The Ely House, like others along the street, was looted by rampaging Union soldiers after the battle, but it survived the ordeal with the same stately character that it manifests today.

The current owners of the mansion, Ruth and Larry Kinsolving, are perfect for their roles as hosts and protectors of the historic landmark. They meticulously care not only for the house and its grounds, but for the history, legends and stories associated with it. They and their ghost-detecting dog, Beau, have a special affection for the apparition. Well, at least the Kinsolvings have a special affection for the ghost. Beau is not so sure.

Larry Kinsolving explained in an email to the author on September 29, 2012:

...We had heard that prior encounters occurred in the upstairs hallway or at the head of the stairs. The prior owner saw her at the top of the stairs. But we have been in the house four years now and have personally observed little that might be connected to the presence of a ghost. There were faucets that were found running and the usual misplaced items for which we spent a lot of time searching but those things seem to happen in all households and do not prove the presence of a ghost. We have noticed however that Beau our male standard poodle has on several evening occasions become very agitated while we were in our upstairs family room that has a direct view of the hallway and the head of the stairs.[3]

Beau, it should be mentioned, is a big and friendly dog. He loves attention and is always quick to greet guests to the house. The ghost, however, has never ranked on his list of favorite visitors:

...He would tuck his tail between his legs and stare down the hallway. It would be obvious that his complete attention was being captured. He would not bark but every few minutes he would circle the coffee table and then resume his staring while always making sure he was standing between the hallway and us. Later when we would head down the hallway on our way to the bedroom, Beau would get in front of us, brace back against us as if to slow us down but with his eyes riveted on the same spot in the hallway. Our other standard poodle, Abby, was oblivious to whatever was capturing Beau's attention.[4]

Dogs, in fact, are often very sensitive to things that humans can neither see nor hear. Their barking sometimes foretells earthquakes, they hear sounds that are inaudible to human ears, and often they can sense evil or bad-intent coming from a would-be attacker. Can they also see ghosts? Many people believe that they can.

An encounter that took place in the house in September 2012 provides fascinating evidence. Ruth had just gone down to the kitchen for water, leaving Larry and Beau in the upstairs family room, when something very strange began to take place:

...Soon after she left, Beau jumped up from his usual sleeping position and started staring down the hallway, tail between his legs. As I watched Beau, I knew he must be seeing the ghost again and regretted my camera was not handy to record his reaction as you had requested us to do. Then I looked up from Beau and was startled to actually see the ghost in the hallway just behind the banister down where our grandfather clock is located. My first reaction was that this really couldn't be happening. But it was, and I was delighted.[5]

It is interesting to note that the ghost appeared on September 25, 2012, just two days from the 148th anniversary of the Battle of Marianna. Since her story is sometimes tied to the battle, could her appearances be tied to its anniversary date?

Larry Kinsolving's first encounter with the ghost of the Ely-Criglar Mansion was remarkable and more than a bit unsettling:

...The ghost's image was not sharp and clear like viewing a real person standing there would be. But it was distinguishable and there seemed to be a

source of faint light within her image which I did not really notice until she was gone. She was standing but I do not remember noticing either hands or feet. Her image seemed to fade away towards her right. Her facial features were not clear and I was not aware of seeing any hair. I have described the ghost as a female but that may have been influenced by the fact that I expected our ghost to be a woman. But I do not remember seeing any distinguishing form except that the image was dressed in what could be described in the same terms as the ghost described by the former owner of the house and the woman in my recurring dream – a white high-necked blouse and a long dark colored skirt. The encounter was very short, only seconds.[6]

After watching in stunned silence until the apparition disappeared, Larry found his voice and called out that she would always be welcome in the house. When Ruth returned from the kitchen a few seconds later, she found Larry and Beau still staring at the spot where the ghost had manifested herself.

Other residents of the house have told similar stories over the years, going back many decades. There has been some speculation that the ghost might be the apparition of a beautiful young woman brought back from Louisiana for service as a house slave by Francis Ely during the years before the Civil War. Marianna tradition holds that she was the most beautiful woman ever seen by many in the city. There also has been speculation that the she might be one of the female members of the Ely family from years past. The family lost most of its fortune in the Civil War and John R. Ely, son of the home's builder, was a key figure in the Reconstruction War that erupted in Jackson County from 1866-1876. His son, John R. Ely, Jr., was lynched by a mob in northeastern Jackson County after paying too much attention to the young daughter of the owner of the old mill on Irwin's Mill Creek. The Ely family had more than its share of tragedy over the years and the ghost is undoubtedly connected to some part of it.

Or perhaps she just loves the beautiful old home so much that she has never been able to fully tear herself from it.

---

[1] To learn more, please see Dale Cox, *The Battle of Marianna, Florida (Expanded Edition)*, 2011.
[2] Personal Communication, Ruth and Larry Kinsolving, 2012; Personal Inspection, 2012.
[3] Personal Communication, Larry Kinsolving, September 29, 2012.
[4] *Ibid.*
[5] *Ibid.*

---

[6] *Ibid.*

Chapter Fifteen

The Aycock Ghosts

IN OCTOBER OF 1905, NEWSPAPER READERS ACROSS THE NATION learned with horror that one of the largest mass murders in Florida history had been enacted at a logging camp just west of the Jackson County community of Steele City. The incident claimed the lives of eight county inmates and a man employed to stand watch over them. Some believe that the victims of the tragedy still linger near the scene of their deaths.

On visiting the site today, it is difficult to imagine the horror once enacted there. The surrounding scene is one of farms and woods, with no visible trace remaining of the camp where the crime took place. Few people in the vicinity know the horrible history associated with the site or of the ghostly figures said to haunt the woods there. Truth be told, however, if there is any place in Jackson County with the tragic potential for a real mass haunting, this is it.

The story of the Aycock Ghosts begins with the purchase of a vast tract of timberland in the area by the Aycock Brothers of Georgia. Already well-known lumber barons, the Aycocks lived in the city of Moultrie but chartered their Florida operation in nearby Cordele in 1904:

...Application for a charter for the Aycock Bros. Lumber Co., composed of W.E. and T.J. Aycock and Evans Reynolds, has been filed with the county clerk. The capital stock of the proposed corporation is to be $50,000. The main office will be

in Cordele, but the principal operations of the company's manufacturing department will be in Florida.[1]

Construction began almost immediately on an industrial complex at the small railroad siding of Allie, located four miles due west of Cottondale on the L&N Railroad between that town and Chipley. It was the railroad, in fact, that had drawn the attention of the Aycock Brothers to the site. The trains provided a way for them to get their lumber and rosin out of the woods and to market. By the spring of 1905, construction of the massive plant at Allie was almost finished:

The Aycock Bros. Lumber Co. have now nearly completed their large saw mill at Allie, six miles east of town (i.e. Chipley). This will be one of the largest and most modern saw mills in West Florida with a cutting capacity of one hundred thousand feet per day. With three large brick dry kilns and a big planning mill they will work about 150 hands.[2]

Even today, an operation of the size and scope of the Aycock mill would be considered impressive. The initial hiring of 150 hands to run the mill and harvest the timber also created the need to house them, preferably on-site. The firm handled this by building one of the largest "company towns" ever constructed in Jackson County. In addition to homes for perhaps 500 people (workers and their families), the community also included stores, a railroad station and a post office as well as the various mills and other facilities associated with the company's operations.

With the completion of its houses, stores, sawmill, drying kilns, railroad station and planning mill, it was logical that the company owners would stamp their name on the community itself. Allie ceased to exist and on May 31, 1905, the *Pensacola Journal* reported that, "The Aycock Bros. Lumber Co. have changed the name of the post office and telegraph office and railroad station to Aycock, Fla."[3]

To support the industrial facilities at Aycock, the company built or acquired a system of logging roads, a naval stores camp and a small railroad that ran south from the L&N tracks for about ten miles through the edge of Washington County and then back into Jackson County again. It carried rosin and timber from the outlying naval stores camp west of Steele City and just north of Alford to the main complex at Aycock.[4]

Although they hired more than 150 people to run their operation, the Aycock brothers were as interested in securing cheap labor as other timber barons of their day. An opportunity presented itself to them in the form of the convict labor leasing practice then in operation across much of Florida.

The convict leasing system had been initiated in 1877 and allowed counties to lease convicts from their jails to private businesses. The money gained from the practice went into the county Road & Bridge Fund and was a vital source of revenue for local government. The practice also eliminated the need for counties to maintain large jail facilities, since the employers leasing the inmates were responsible for housing and feeding them.

The Aycock brothers entered almost immediately into leasing contracts with the Board of County Commissioners for Jackson County. The use of convict labor may even have been part of their business plan before they ever started building their company town west of Cottondale. To house the inmates turned over to them, they established two convict stockades: one on the grounds of the main operation at Aycock and the other 10 miles south down the logging railroad at the remote naval stores camp. These locations allowed the company to house convicts at both ends of their massive 25,000 acre timber tract. Both stockades, generally described as wood-frame buildings, were finished and in use by the end of the summer of 1905.

The convict leasing system was not without its critics. The early 1900s were a time of great social reform in the nation and newspaper editors and private citizens alike railed against the system, which they equated with slavery. Counties were literally leasing human beings to private companies and these individuals were then worked, often in substandard conditions, with no choice in the matter and receiving no compensation for their labors.

The conditions at the Aycock stockades were far from ideal. Not only were the convicts worked long hours under harsh and dangerous conditions, they were chained inside the stockades at night to eliminate any possibility of escape. It was a recipe for disaster and that is exactly what happened in the early fall of 1905:

On the night of October 7, Aycock Brothers Lumber Co. convict camp burned in Jackson County. In this fire, James Longino, the guard on duty, and eight convicts, were burned to death. Four or five of the bodies were cremated. The only two remaining victims...barely escaped with their lives and are now lying in Aycock's stockade at Aycock, Florida, in a badly burned condition.[5]

One of the two survivors, identified as William McCoy, was so severely injured that there seemed but little chance that he would recover. His escape, and that of his fellow survivor, was gruesome almost beyond imagination:

I remember hearing how some of them climbed as far as their leg chains would let them through the windows and begged witnesses to cut off a foot to free them from their chains and from being burned alive.[6]

News of the fire stunned people in Jackson and Washington Counties and as the story spread, the nation was equally appalled. The cause was first thought to be accidental, with speculation focusing on the explosion of a faulty oil lamp. The theory was so convincing, in fact, that a coroner's inquest was considered unnecessary.

Information came to light over the coming days, however, that quickly changed opinions about the fire. Alarmed by the horrible tragedy and undoubtedly concerned over their own liability in the matter, the Aycock brothers hired a private detective from Chipley named Tom Watts to look into the fire. Watts had established a reputation investigating cases of fraud against the L&N Railroad and quickly became convinced that the fire was not accidental at all, but was "one of the most horrible crimes ever committed in the state."[7]

Watts discovered something that the failure to empanel a coroner's inquest had prevented from emerging already: the heads of James Longino, the guard over the stockade, and an unidentified convict had been smashed with a blunt object. Sam Jones, a misdemeanor convict who served as the trusty of the camp, told the detective that he had seen a man named Jim Glassco enter the guardroom at the entrance of the stockade. A few seconds later he heard two heavy blows, saw fire suddenly rise up from the building and then watched Glassco come out and run away.[8]

Convinced that Glassco was involved in starting the fire, Watts arrested him and took him first to the Washington County Jail in Chipley. From there the suspect was carried by rail to the Jackson County Jail in Marianna:

I find the motive for the crime to have been robbery. Longino had on his person $48.10 and the convict had $5. Longino had drawn a gun (for cause) on Glassco the same night of the fire. The weapon used by Glassco was a spike maul, such as commonly used by railroad trackmen.[9]

A first appearance was held for Glassco at the courthouse in Marianna and the county grand jury was ordered to convene. Although Detective Watts believed that a "strong case was made out" against the suspect, the grand jury did not agree. No indictment was returned against Glassco and the grand jurors instead recommended that the county commission cancel the Aycock Brothers' contract and do everything possible to bring those responsible to justice..

One of the Jackson County Commissioners, J.M. Barnes, went out to the naval stores camp to view the scene of the fire firsthand. After conducting a brief investigation of his own, he determined that "whiskey was very much in evidence." It was his conclusion that the "guard being drunk probably caused the fire." Strangely, there is no indication in county records that the Sheriff of Jackson County was ever asked to investigate the matter.[10]

Detective Watts, as might have been expected, vehemently disagreed with Commissioner Barnes. He wrote to Governor N.B. Broward in Tallahassee, calling for a state investigation. Expressing his belief that eyewitness Sam Jones was somehow involved in the crime, the company detective warned that time was of the essence:

The scene of this terrible crime is some ten miles from the railroad in the logging woods of the lumber company. There is much yet to be learned in this case by careful investigation, and I am sure you will appreciate the importance of looking into the matter fully.

The witnesses, some of them, have already scattered off – one of the most important ones now being in Atlanta, Georgia.[11]

The company detective expressed his view of the incident plainly to Governor Broward, "I regard this as being one of the most horrible crimes ever committed in the state."

The determined detective's efforts aside, no justice was ever obtained for the nine men who died as a result of the terrible fire at the Aycock Brothers naval stores camp. Their bodies were taken up the logging railroad to the main community of Aycock where they were buried in a now forgotten plot by the L&N (today's CSX) Railroad. The most any of the fatally injured men ever got from the county or the Aycock company was the money paid to the doctor who amputated their legs in an unsuccessful effort to save their lives after axes had been used to cut off their feet so they could be pulled away from the chains that attached them to the burning building. Dr. J.S. McGeachy of Chipley was paid $624 for "amputating Six Legs, Visits, Dressing."[12]

The survivors of the tragedy, along with the family members of some of the dead, brought suit in federal court against Aycock Brothers Lumber Company for their losses. John Bryant, who had lost his feet when they were cut off to free him from his chains, sued the company for $25,000, as did the families of several of the others. After two years, the Aycock Brothers settled with Bryant for $5,000. Of that amount, $1,500 went to the lawyers who represented him. The unfortunate former convict received $3,500, the apparent value the parties agreed to place on the legs and feet he left behind at the naval stores camp:

Upon a consultation of the counsel for the plantiffs and defendants to these suits a compromise was effected by the company paying to Bryant and the other plaintiffs a sum of $3,500 and bearing the costs of the litigation. The suits were based upon injuries received by Brant and the deaths of a number of convicts in a stockade, which was destroyed by fire a year ago. Relatives of some of the men burned to death in the stockade, brought actions for damages, but settled for very small amounts.[13]

At the time the Aycock Brothers paid John Bryant $3,500 for the loss of his feet, their company was worth roughly $500,000. In fact, their mill town four miles west of Cottondale continued to thrive for a number of years, at one point even boasting a jewelry store. The old growth longleaf pines were finally all harvested, though, and Aycock faded into history like so many of the Florida Panhandle's other sawmill towns. Not a single building stands today.

Aycock may have faded away, but the terrible tragedy enacted 10 miles south of the town lingers. The publicity over the fire helped end the practice of convict leasing in Florida and elsewhere, but no formal law enforcement investigation of the incident ever took place. Was it mass murder, as Detective Watts believed? Or was it a case of drunkenness gone bad, as a Jackson County Commissioner concluded? No one can really say. As late as 2012, when forensic anthropologists were investigating a known cemetery on the former Dozier School property in Marianna, they expressed no interest in the nine bodies buried in unmarked graves by the railroad tracks at Aycock. Dr. Erin Kimmerle of the University of South Florida became just the latest governmental entity in a long line to express a callous lack of interest in finding the truth about the deaths of nine men who left this world in the most agonizing way imaginable.

Perhaps it is this lack of concern as to their fate that keeps those unfortunate men lingering close to the place they died. Local legend holds that both the old naval stores camp site, where the tragedy took place, and the cemetery where the unfortunate men lay buried are haunted by their spirits. At the secluded stockade site, it is said that the ghosts of the dead still walk in the night. Shadowy figures have been seen moving through the trees and on certain nights it is said that the moans of dying men can be distinctly heard echoing through the bays and swamps.

At Aycock itself, legend holds that blue lights can be seen in the night at the spot where most of the unfortunate victims were buried. The graves themselves are unmarked, even though the men were the prisoners of Jackson County and under its protection at the time they died. The simple wooden markers placed on the graves by coworkers rotted away long ago.

Some believe that the ghosts appear in two different places because their legs and feet rest in the dirt at the site of the naval stores camp, while the rest of their bodies lay forgotten under the dirt of Aycock itself. Perhaps they continue to appear because justice for them has never been done? And as of today, it seems most likely that the world will never know what really happened to the Aycock prisoners that night long ago in the Florida pines.

---

[1] Augusta Chronicle, September 20, 1904, p. 4.

[2] Pensacola Journal, April 19, 1905, p. 1.

[3] Pensacola Journal, May 31, 1905.

[4] E.W. Carswell, *Washington: Florida's Twelfth County*, 1991, p. 313.

[5] Tom Watts to Governor Napoleon B. Broward, October 1905, Carswell Collection.

[6] Gilbert Keener, Washington County Commissioner, 1978, quoted by E.W. Carswell, *Washington: Florida's Twelfth County*, p. 313.

[7] Watts to Broward, October 1905.

[8] *Ibid.*

[9] *Ibid.*

[10] J.M. Barnes, quoted by E.W. Carswell, *Washington: Florida's Twelfth County*, p. 315.

[11] Tom Watts to Gov. Napoleon B. Broward, Octonber 1905, Carswell Collection.

[12] Bill of Dr. J.S. McGeachy, November 6, 1905, Jackson County Archives.

[13] Montgomery *Advertiser*, March 14, 1907, p. 5.

Chapter Sixteen
Other Stories

THE LEGEND OF THE GHOST OF BELLAMY BRIDGE and the nine other stories related in this book are not the only tales of the supernatural or of strange creatures that can be heard in Jackson County, Florida. There are many others.

The third oldest county in Florida and with a human history that dates back thousands of years, Jackson County has produced a wide array of legends and stories of strangeness over the years. Here are some of the more interesting ones for which sufficient information could not be located to create a full chapter. They are some of the "best of the rest."

Orange Eyes – This bizarre little story was told by teenagers around Marianna in 2012. According to them, there is a place near the overpass where Highway 73 crosses I-10 that has become a popular location for seeing a ghost. By pulling off 73 and down a dirt road that runs near the overpass, it is said that a pair of orange eyes can be seen in the rearview mirror, as if something is following the car.

The Granberry Mansion – Once located on Hartsfield Road, the historic Granberry Mansion was built by the Blackshear family long before the Civil War. Famously haunted, it fell into disrepair and burned to the ground during the late 20th century.

Old Graceville City Hall – Employees of the city of Graceville maintained that the second floor of the old city hall was haunted by the ghost of a former police chief. He was seen there a number of times over the years by a wide array of credible eyewitnesses. City offices have since been moved to a new location, although not because of the ghost.

Byrd Cemetery – Located on River Road north of Sneads, Byrd Cemetery was a small family burial ground with graves dating as far back as the antebellum era. It was bulldozed during the 1980s. A family member found a broken tombstone there and carried it home, only to experience so many abnormal occurrences in and around his house (including the toppling of porcelain birds from a shelf) that it was decided to take the stone back to its original place. The incidents stopped when the marker was returned.

Hayes-Long Mansion – This beautiful antebellum home is a private residence on Highway 71 North in Greenwood. Some former occupants have reported encounters with the ghostly apparition of a slave, while others say they experienced no issues with the supernatural while they lived in the house.

Holden House – Located on Lafayette Street in Marianna, this old antebellum home was the residence of General William E. Anderson of the Florida Militia before and during the Civil War. Local tradition holds that it is haunted by a playful ghost that likes to move things around during the night when the structure is otherwise unoccupied.

The Campbellton Creature – A Bigfoot or Sasquatch, this monster was repeatedly observed in an area near Campbellton and in the vicinity of today's Spring Hill Landfill during the 1950s and 1960s.

The Bellamy Booger – Another story associated with the Bellamy Bridge vicinity, this monster is said to be a Bigfoot or Sasquatch that has been seen in the floodplain swamps between Bellamy Bridge and the Florida Caverns. It may be identical with the "Campbellton Creature."

The Monkeys of Godwin Lake – Fishermen returning from the slough that leads north from Buena Vista Landing on Lake Seminole have reported seeing and hearing a family of monkeys in the trees around Godwin Lake. They have yet to be photographed, but considering the way monkeys and pythons have been spreading north in Florida, it is certainly possible.

Tie-Snake Hole – An old legend holds that a deep hole in the Chattahoochee River near the site of Econchattimico's Reservation (1823-1838) is the home of the infamous "Tie-Snakes" of Creek Indian legend. The Tie-Snakes would grab a person unfortunate enough to fall into the river at the site and wrap themselves around him. Their victim would then be carried down to the "Tie-Snake King," a monstrous snake of enormous size, who would decide whether the captive would be released or forced to remain and become a Tie-Snake himself.

Ghost of the Florida Caverns – Photographs taken of tour groups inside the tour cave at Florida Caverns State Park are said to sometimes show the ghost of a much-loved park ranger.

Rip Van Winkle of Jackson County – A Cincinnati newspaper reported during the 19th century that a sleeping man had been found in the Natural Bridge Cavern (today's Indian Cave) at Florida Caverns State Park. He claimed to have been there for more than 100 years.

Photographs

Ghosts & Monsters of Jackson County

Russ House in Marianna, Florida

St. Luke's Episcopal Church in Marianna, Florida

Beau spots the Ghost of the Ely-Criglar House
Courtesy of Ruth & Larry Kinsolving

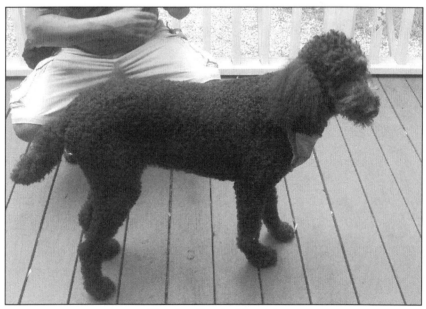

Beau in a Happier Moment

Larry Kinsolving welcomes Military Officers to the Ely-Criglar Mansion

Ely-Criglar Mansion in Marianna

Where Larry & Beau saw the Ghost in the Ely-Criglar Mansion

Inside the Ely-Criglar Mansion

Ocheesee Pond, Where the "Wild Man" was Captured

Ocheesee Pond: Was a Bigfoot captured here?

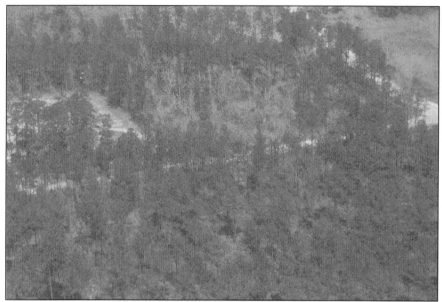

Scene of the last sighting of the Two Egg Stump Jumper

The Ghost of Central School at Old Parramore

One-Room School at Old Parramore

Crumbling Tobacco Barn at Old Parramore

The Holden House in Marianna, Home of a Playful Ghost

St. Luke's Episcopal Church in Marianna, Florida

References

Books

Mary Lawrence Beeman, "Killed in Cold Blood," *Our Women in the War: The Lives They Lived, The Deaths They Died*, published by the Charleston News and Courier, 1885.

Carswell, E.W., *Washington: Florida's Twelfth County*, Chipley, Florida, 1991.

Cox, Dale, *Old Parramore: The History of a Florida Ghost Town*, Bascom, Florida, 2010.

- *The Battle of Marianna, Florida* (Expanded Edition), Bascom, Florida, 2011.

- *The History of Jackson County, Florida: The Early Years* (Volume 1), Bascom, Florida, 2008.

Florida Law Journal, Volume IX, Number 5, May 1935.

Hentz, Caroline Lee, *Marcus Warland or the Long Moss Spring*, 1853.

Papy, Mario D., *Cases Argued and Adjudged in the Supreme Court of Florida at Terms Held in 1855*, Volume VI, Number 1, Tallahassee, Office of the *Florida Sentinel*, Printed by Benjamin F. Allen, 1855.

Articles

Mark F. Boyd, "The Expedition of Marcos Delgado from Apalache to the Upper Creek Country in 1686," *Florida Historical Quarterly*, Volume XVI, Number 1, July 1937.

Portier, Rt. Rev. Michael, "From Pensacola to St. Augustine in 1827: A Journey of the Rt. Rev. Michael Portier," *Florida Historical Quarterly*, Volume XVI, Number 2, October 1937.

Armstrong Purdee, "Eyewitness Tells of Burning of Church," *The Kalender*, June 1, 1931.

Newspapers

Augusta Chronicle, 1904.

Camden Gazette, 1818.

Montgomery Advertiser, 1907.

Pensacola Journal, 1905.

Providence Patriot, 1823.

Tallahassee *Floridian*, 1837, 1838.

The New York Times, 1910, 1884.

Toledo Blade, 1910.

Manuscripts

Barreda, Rodrigo de la, "Journal," 1693 (Copy in Private Collection of the Author).

Bond for Construction of Bridge executed by Bird B. Hathaway, Horace Ely & Others, January 10, 1852, Jackson County Archives.

Pearl Cox, "Cox Family: Charles W. and Ola Avery," Book Three in a series of unpublished volumes on the Cox family lineage, n.d.

Croom, Hardy Bryan, to Wife, Decemebr 6, 1836, Croom Family Papers, University of North Carolina.

Indenture between Samuel C. Bellamy and Edward C. Bellamy, November 19, 1844, Jackson County Archives.

Jackson County Commission Minutes, 1850, 1851, 1872, 1874, 1911, 1914, Jackson County Archives.

Kinsolving, Larry, to Dale Cox, September 29, 2012.

References

McGeacy, Dr. J.S., Bill for Services, November 6, 1905, Jackson County Archives.

Registration Form for First American Road in Florida, National Register of Historic Places, National Park Service, Washington, D.C., Received August 17, 1988.

Watts, Tom, to Governor Napoleon B. Broward, October 1905, Carswell Collection.

Index

Jack, 89
Littleton, 89
National Register of Historic Places, 107
Natural Bridge Cavern, 123
Natural Bridge of the Chipola, 42
Natural Bridge of the Chipola River, 47
Neal's Landing, 44, 46
Neal's Landing Park, 43
New England, 15
New York, 4, 85
Newington Plantation, 10
Nickels
  Woody, 89, 90
Nickel's Inn, 4
Noah, 2
Noah's Ark, 2
North Carolina, 1, 2, 7, 8, 9, 10, 11, 15, 21
Northwest Florida Water Management District, 45, 66
Norwood
  Jesse J., 109
Nubbin Ridge Cemetery, 52
Nubbin Ridge Road, 53
Oak Grove Road, 78, 97
Ocheesee Pond, 84, 85
Ohio, 21, 82
Oklahoma, 46, 82
Oregon, 84
Outer Banks, 15
Parramore, 53, 79, 97, 98, 99, 100, 101, 102
Parramore Landing Park, 53
Parramore Road, 53, 97
Parramore School, 100
Pascofa, 82
Peacock
  Frank, 52
Peacock Bridge, 54
Pearl Harbor, 98
Pensacola, 43, 82

Pensacola Bay, 87
Peri Landing, 52, 98, 104
Peters
  Doc, 74
Pettaway
  William R., 49
Pine Level Cemetery, 99
Planter's Northern Bride, 21
Port Jackson, 46, 49
Port St. Joe, 47
Portier
  Rt.Rev. Michael, 12
Purdee
  Armstrong, 89
Quincy, 9
Raiford, 30
Reconstruction, 51
Red Ground. *See* Ekanachatte
Red Stick Creeks, 44
Red Sticks
  Creek Indians, 44
Reynolds
  Evans, 113
Rip Van Winkle, 123
River Road, 122
Robinson
  Dr. Henry, 90
  Henry, 50
  Henry J., 98
Rock Arch Cave, 11, 12
Rock Cave Plantation, 11, 12, 13, 14, 15, 17
Rocky Comfort, 11
Russ
  Joseph W., Jr., 93
Russ House, 93
Russ Street, 93
Sam Smith Cave, 11
San Antonio, 40, 43
Sanders
  R.A., 88
Sanders Gang, 50
Savannah, 46

Books by Dale Cox

www.exploresouthernhistory.com/books

Books for Kindle by Dale Cox

www.exploresouthernhistory.com/kindle

Made in the USA
Columbia, SC
24 February 2025

54252605R00093